Back to Ourselves

Introduction to a New World Era

Amitai Rosengart

ISBN: 1720464235
ISBN-13: 978-1720464235

CONTENTS

Acknowledgments

1   Chapter 1 – Introduction to the 21st century

We are one   Pg 6

The cognitive revolution   Pg 9

It all begins with the words   Pg 16

It's all about education   Pg 26

Equality and freedom   Pg 36

2   Chapter 2- Economy and Politics

Introduction to the 21st century   Pg 48

Ideas about governments and politics   Pg 52

The professional governing model   Pg 58

Early Capitalism and our monetary system   Pg 64

The era of Social capitalism   Pg 66

The outcome of establishing a profit structure   Pg 78

Import and export: Good tools in the wrong hands   Pg 88

Capitalism and government   Pg 89

Looking forward   Pg 99

3   Chapter 3 – Society, Values and Social Movements

Human Nature   Pg 108

Strong societies require strong individuals   Pg 115

CONTENTS

Acknowledgments

1   Chapter 1 – Introduction to the 21st century

     We are one   Pg 6

     The cognitive revolution   Pg 9

     It all begins with the words   Pg 16

     It's all about education   Pg 26

     Equality and freedom   Pg 36

2   Chapter 2- Economy and Politics

     Introduction to the 21st century   Pg 48

     Ideas about governments and politics   Pg 52

     The professional governing model   Pg 58

     Early Capitalism and our monetary system   Pg 64

     The era of Social capitalism   Pg 66

     The outcome of establishing a profit structure   Pg 78

     Import and export: Good tools in the wrong hands   Pg 88

     Capitalism and government   Pg 89

     Looking forward   Pg 99

3   Chapter 3 – Society, Values and Social Movements

     Human Nature   Pg 108

     Strong societies require strong individuals   Pg 115

The technological evolution and it implications   Pg 120

Individualism   Pg 123

The chronicle of social change   Pg 130

Time for social change   Pg 147

Epilogue

Resources and additional reading

Anything written in those pages is neither my invention nor the creation of a single mind. You will find ideas and texts that are not mine alone, but the work of intellectual giants I'm lucky to stand on the shoulders of. The capacity of our generation to realize where we are standing is only thanks to the great minds that have manifested ideas and shaped societies throughout mankind's history. I do not have the capacity or memory to recall where all the information is coming from and hope that at least one new conclusion will be taken and implied from this book for the sake of a better society. At the end of the book, you will find references to many books that contain the basic concepts and ideas described here.

Back to Ourselves

Today, it is known and agreed that we have enough resources to maintain humanity as a species, while promoting the well-being of the planet and all its inhabitants. We have the capacity to promise peace, education and safety to all.

So, why are we still busy killing each other?

Chapter 1:

Introduction to the 21st century

We Are One

Welcome to the new world era. Thank you for taking the time to understand what we all know but forgot how to see.

Like many of you, I enjoy the comfort of life in the Western world, one attached to words like progress, freedom, equality—and terror. For many years, I enjoyed all this world could give me. I travelled around the world and lived in many European countries. This world we live in, preaches fear of the unknown and controls us by manipulating the memories of our past for the sake of having small moments in live enjoyed in the security of our families and the tranquility of our daily routines.

As I'm sitting and writing in the tranquility of western Europe, foreign fighters scream orders of massacre into the air and people armed with guns fight for the sake of ideas that are not their own. Those soldiers, who are our children, are poisoned by fear of a reality far from existence. They go into the world and blindly spread doctrines that separate humanity instead of connecting us.

We live in a world where the words used to inspire us as individuals and gather us as communities have become the tools of terror and fear holding us captive in our own existence. They're used not by far-off organizations we've never seen, but by our own governments and superiors. But, those willing to listen hear the truth behind those words. And the truth is, something is terribly wrong in our society. Cruelty, injustice, intolerance, and oppression are just a small part of the society we so proudly call the Western culture.

Where we once had the freedom to object, think, and express reactions to ideas, we now have blind consensus and a surveillance system to challenge our comfort and solicit our submission. Asking how this happened is a good foundational question to understand where we come from, but it's the wrong question if we're searching for someone to blame for this change in society. In this case, *how* this happened becomes a substitute for *who* let this happen, and the answer is an uncomfortable truth: ourselves.

There are certainly those more responsible for this change than others, but if you're looking for the guilty one to blame, you need only to look in the mirror, both as an individual and as a society. I know why I accepted this order silently: I was blind and ignorant, surrounded by a system that abuses its knowledge not for the sake of promoting the common good, but for maintaining the system's power while ignoring the needs of the planet and all living things.

A system carefully constructed on fear and false reality conspires to corrupt our reason and rob of us our common sense. Fear is a disease. It brings out the worst in us. Our education systems are generations old and teach us to view our past as a dark period filled with poverty, mistakes, and dangers, instead of celebrating the beauty of our evolution and the lessons we've learned along the way. In such an educational system, it's hard for an individual to understand who they are, which makes it harder to understand their role in the society. There is a big difference between knowing where we came from—which is basic knowledge to all humans—and knowing why things turned out the way they did.

Education that teaches the young to be terrified, full of

guilt and hate contributes to their separation from their peers around the world, and doesn't promote progress or a society that sustains individuals. Misconceptions about our society stem from the lack of communication between individuals, something we've struggled with since the dawn of civilization. The world is changing. Improvements to our communication technology in the last decade now allow individuals all over the world to communicate in a manner of seconds with minimal effort. This technological evolution and its integration into the mass market is a major step towards a positive globalization. However, in the wrong hands, it can easily become a tool used for controlling the masses and promoting fear and separation.

The general feeling of the individual, that something in his reality is deeply wrong, is a step toward the realization that we must find a better solution for our modern societal problems. As the educational system has taught us mainly what is right and not *why* it's right, our society is no longer capable of articulating the problem and its cause. We all know it and we all feel it: something is terribly wrong in the reality we are all living in. We see it in our economies, political structures, and social systems. But, none of us can describe it. Hopefully, by examining the reality from a new perspective, we will start to understand these problems. We will not only understand what went wrong, but also what lessons we can learn that will help us build a new system for our increasingly global society. Globalization is a natural and positive process. Any attempted to fight it is unproductive. It is the way we will decide to build it that will determine the future of our children and our societies. We can and should do better. It is not hard as it looks, it just requires motivated individuals, arms with the right tools, willing to get out of their comfort zone and do a bit more for their societies. The future is in our hand and only we can promise a better world for our children. This is what this book is all about.

It is important to note that our evolution by itself is neither good or bad. Evolution is a natural process which comes hand-in-hand with life. Making bad decisions is an inevitable and a healthy part of the process of decision making. It's an integral part of the process of trial and error. The belief that we don't have choices or alternatives comes from ignorance, led by our superiors and sometimes by ourselves for momentary peace. Let's try to be better than ourselves for a while, not because we need to but because we can. We are living this life and we will shape the future for our children.

We're being given a chance, and it would be a shame not to take it.

The Cognitive Revolution

To understand the reality, we are living in and build a foundation for a positive social change, we must touch on multiple fields of study and challenge core beliefs.

Humanity's culture has changed rapidly over the last 300 years. As a species, we've been expanding geographically for at least 30,000 years. Based on recent studies, scientists agree that humans also gained modern levels of intelligence around the same time period. Trying to understand who we are by only examining 2,500 years of history will yield poor conclusions. Homo sapiens—our species—have been evolving for the last 70,000 years and have conquered the majority of the world in just the last 12,000 years.

That may sound surprising, as we generally only learn the last 3000-5000 years of history in school, and this gives us some narrow tools for the understanding of our progress and who we are. This limited education that teaches us so little about our past naturally leads us to think that, compared to the rest of the planet evolving around us, our intellectual capacity is quite new and still evolving. The truth is, our intellect as an individual sapience (the professional term to describe human being) did not evolve for a very long time. It is quite safe to say, then, that for at least 12,000 years, our intellectual capabilities have not increased as a species.

You may be feeling something strange now, and that's normal. The information presented above contradicts the basics beliefs you have been taught your whole life. I had the same reaction. It's easy to ignore and throw away information we feel uncomfortable with, but that doesn't make the information less relevant or true.

The main reason this information is hard to accept is because we've been taught that over the last 3,000 years, society's progress is the result of a few intelligent people and the evolution of our species. Indeed, humanity has developed a lot in the last 3,000 years, but as we will see, those changes didn't require a jump in the intellectual capacity of humans.

So, what changed from those early stages of humanity? What tools did we acquire that helped us conquer the world? The answer is quite simple: Communication.

Comparing modern humans to our ancient ancestors helps us understand how we evolved *and* how we didn't. As we are the result of evolution, both our capabilities and shortcomings are attached to the world around us. This unique combination has made us who we are today. By looking at what we've become over the millennia, we can try to understand what traits we don't need and what we have gained.

Modern humans are unlikely to survive isolated in a jungle compared to our 3,000-year-old ancestors. It is an important point, as it can teach us many things. First, during the evolutionary process, we lost the majority of our physical capacities as animals surviving in nature. Our physical evolution occurred parallel to the evolution of technology and our capacity to affect and control our surroundings. Today, much of Western society lives in cities far removed from our natural habitat, and this evolution has caused us to lose many basic survival instincts from the previous millennia. For example, more people require glasses, and the majority of the Western world suffers from certain back problems. Our ability to map out our surroundings and survive without a nearby supermarket is low. Looking at it straight forward, it can be said that humans are losing their capacity to live and survive in their natural habitat – The nature.

Most tools we use daily—wheels, forks, chairs, tables, clothes, umbrellas, and others—were invented hundreds or thousands of years ago. They haven't changed much since then. Those tools are no less important than they were the day of their invention, but that does not contradict the argument about evolution.

It's not that we are not evolving, but that the evolution of humans isn't contingent on bigger brains, more intellect, or more physical strength as we like to believe. We did evolve, fast and everywhere, and the simplest explanation for our global conquest is to look at our social and mental development over the last 30,000 years. During this period, humans have constantly worked on developing a new tool we didn't have before: the tool of communication, both verbal and written. Communication is our strongest tool, which brought us from being part of nature to surpassing it. Thanks to our evolved communication, humans have conquered and settled all over the world, allowing us to build new, strong cultures. One of the easiest way to see this evolution, is by observing the characteristics of our leaders. Over the last 3,000 years, humanity's greatest leaders have become the best communicators in their respective societies, not the strongest or fastest. As those traits became less relevant to one survival.

Let's examine this more deeply. Before the communication revolution, humans lived in small packs—not that different from other animals. Their communication capacity was limited, and they lived mainly in the moment, merely reacting to the world around them. The religions of that period were based on the fundamental idea that humans are part of the nature and not its controller. Historians have concluded that in this pre-communication period, the capacity for homo sapiens to group up and plan ahead was limited. This prevented our species from planning or organizing large-scale movements and societies, which made us weak compared to the physical size, speed, and force of potential predators like lions, tigers, mammoths and wolves.

Humans evolved to be social animals, a trait observed in all groups of mammals that are too weak individually. This social need evolved to provide security and comfort. As homo sapiens were at a big disadvantage compared to potential predators, it's not surprising that the tool evolved by human to overcome predators and dominate the planet came from something other than physical speed or size. Our capacity to communicate allows us to share ideas, evolve them as a group, and maintain them as a society. Since then, our capacity for communication has continued to develop, allowing humans as a species to create bigger communities, larger concepts, and acquire a deeper understanding of the world we live in.

The communication revolution has affected many aspects of human life. It gave us tools that forever changed the world. It gave us:

- The capacity to pass information from generation to generation, allowing ideas and concepts to evolve over time. This allows us to save a lot of energy and research, as we inherit the knowledge of our elders regarding what's dangerous and needed, the best way to avoid and/or solve problems, and how to work together to arrive at solutions.
- The capacity to share a set of beliefs with a group. This allows us to create both trust and communities as the more beliefs people have in common, the more comfortable and

safe they feel around each other. This helped humans fight for common goals, but it also helped us justified the massacre of humans who lack our shared beliefs. This result is, without any doubt, one of the strongest forces driving humanity. We see it not only in our day-to-day lives, but in wars and separations based on religion, nationalism, and political parties.

- The capacity to share information and brainstorm as a group. Information sharing and brainstorming were confined to local groups, but developing writing and language systems shared among humans helped spread ideas across greater geographic regions. In many cases the process of brainstorming is used as an accelerator of creativity. The writing of this book is a wonderful example for it.

Understanding that our capacity to evolve from a clan to a village, from a village to a city, and from a city to a country is possible thanks and only due to our ability to communicate, understand abstract concepts, and pass information, is extremely important as it is a fundamental concept repeated over all this book.

Communication developed over time thanks to and with our ability to think and understand in terms separate from the "real world." Abstract thinking allowed humans to create plans, wage better war, create abstract religions, separate people and unite them under certain ideals, develop new surveillance techniques, and made humans the best inventors of tools, stories, and dreams. Put simply, without the ability to imagine and communicate, humans couldn't create large-scale societies or philosophies.

In our modern time, a person in the Western world is mainly occupied by obstructive thoughts, concepts and hopes, as we live in a society in which we work for money we don't see, talk with people we cannot touch, and believe in the ideals that are located only in our mind. We'll explore this deeply throughout all this book.

Understanding that our capacity for abstract thought and communication is neither inherently good nor bad is important. It is just that: a capacity. It's simultaneously the solution for our problems and the cause of our misery, a tool used for both good and bad. Detached from its usage, any tool or capacity is no more than an unused potential. It is our mind and actions that transform it to become what it is.

Another important point we need to agree upon before starting deeper conversations is that for at least 500 years, the biggest danger to humans has come from other humans. We're no longer threatened by other animals; those days are long forgotten by our species. Deadly Plagues are controlled, and starvation exists only due to the lack of positive communication and not a lack of resources. For hundreds of years, the main cause of early death of humans is ourselves. By itself, it's something we're all aware of. Nevertheless, it takes us longer to acknowledge this when we really consider it. For the sake of making this point even more stronger, it can be agreed that in the last 2,000 years, the main cause of mass murder has been in the name of religion, racism, or plain ignorance. The reality is that if we stop being afraid of each other and killing each other, our ability to create, expand upon, and improve our lives will increase exponentially.

For those of you who would like to take more time to investigate this subject, I recommend reading *Sapiens* by Yuval Noah Harari. Our lack of intellectual evolution doesn't mean we've stopped all progress and evolution. Instead, it means we've made progress in other areas.

The human mind is a fascinating thing. It can't know what it's never heard of, but it absorbs any new information available. As a lion born in a cage can't imagine the feeling of running in the nature, a person born in Europe and educated by local beliefs is incapable of imagining alternatives to his education until he meets someone with a different experience.

This point is a very important one, as we tend to see ignorance and stupidity as negatives, not as a basic condition of all humans. Ignorance and stupidity have always been explained by one person with "more" knowledge than another. It's strange, as we all start our life fragile and ignorant of our own existence, without any knowledge of our surroundings. As information can only be obtained from communication and experience, the idea that ignorance or lack of understanding is a negative trait is wrong, and denies one's own original experience. People that treat other people as ignorant as a problem or a negative thing, in the majority of cases, are reflecting the fear and ignorance of themselves. As we all start ignorant of our own existence, judging the incapability of another without helping them gain access to the tools and ideas obtained by the first person, will represent in the majority of the cases the ignorance of the first person and not the incapability of the other.

From the other side, it's true to say that an ignorant society is easier to control and manipulate. The only reason to keep information from a society is to control the population, and there is nothing productive in depriving a society of tools for growth if not for the sake of keeping it weak. Those understandings are not new and have been well-understood by the ruling elite for thousands of years.

As communication channels evolve through the development of the internet and our ability to see the world as it truly is expanding, a new reality has emerged. It's a reality in which we do not need to lean on our leaders' decisions to supply us information as they please, but one in which we can ask questions on a global scale instantly, together monitoring the information and looking for alternative answers. As we look at this information and begin to understand our society, the global population, and the problems emerging from our lifestyle, it forces us to look at the true causes of humanity's problems. All concepts of war, famine, poverty, and division look less and less like a product of nature and more like the pursue of the few after power and profit in the price of the impoverishment and misery of the many.

This dictatorship of the few is close to its end, as we are all human, sharing the same planet, in which there is enough food and space for everybody, without the need to enslave people, animals and destroying the planet.

It All Begins with the Words

Language simultaneously evolves with our capacity for communication. Words are used for all our communicative purposes. We use them to understand the world around us, the people surrounding us, and ourselves. During our conversation about the evolution of our language, it's important to remember that because we talk to ourselves in our own heads using words before we speak to others, the development of our communication was first with ourselves and then with our groups.

Let's start with the definition of what we call a word. In linguistics, a word is the smallest element that can be uttered in isolation with objective or practical meaning. This contrasts deeply with a morpheme, which is the smallest unit of meaning, but will not necessarily stand on its own.

A word may consist of a single morpheme (for example: oh, rock, red, quick, run, expect), or several (rocks, redness, quickly, running, unexpected), whereas a morpheme may not be able to stand on its own as a word (in the words just mentioned, these are -s, -ness, -ly, -ing, un-, -ed, respectively). A complex word typically includes a root and one or more affixes (rock-s, red-ness, quick-ly, run-ning, un-expect-ed), or more than one root in a compound (black-board, sand-box).

Words can be put together to build larger elements of language, such as phrases (a red rock, put up with), clauses (I threw a rock), and sentences (He threw a rock too, but he missed). The term 'word' may refer to a spoken word or to a written word, or sometimes to the abstract concept behind either. Spoken words are made up of units of sound called phonemes, and written words of symbols called graphemes, such as the letters of the English alphabet.

During our conversation about the evolution of words and its direct implication on our daily life, it's important to remember the following concept: words have been created to describe the reality around us, which imply that the reality around us do not require our words or understanding for their continued existence. Things that require words to exist should be categorized as human concepts. As such, it's humans that sustain its existence and not reality itself.

At first, words were developed to signal upcoming dangers to one another in a more efficient and accurate way. For example, the call for a predator arriving from the sky or from the ground is also found in monkeys and other evolved animals. The capacity to signal locations by voice, movement, or smell is found in many animals, as bees, dolphins, wolves, and so on. It's possible that at its first stage of evolution, words served humans as survival tools.

As humans evolved, our ability to communicate in words evolved to signal the dangers of the time period. The words for colors helped us teach other which fruits were dangerous, words to describe past events helped teach lessons between generations, and maybe most importantly, gossiping helped humans learn who they could trust. Without any doubt, the development of new words made the life of the humans of the early period safer and easier.

The new capacity to communicate allow humans to cooperate with bigger groups, get a better understanding of their surroundings, and create collective knowledge.

As we developed words, we also gained the ability to think abstractly. The capacity to think about the future, to plan ahead and create new things requires abstract thought. Abstract thinking is a very useful tool when it is shared with others, as it brings the capacity to create, to predict and to understand better the nature around the group. At its primal development stages, these new capacities were in any standard revolutionary.

When combined, words and abstract thinking helped humans suddenly acquire better tactics for defense and new variations of group attacks to conquer predators, nature and each other. For example, with these new abilities, early humans could describe new animals, threats, and situations to their friends. As long as the first human used terms familiar to others in their group, other humans had the capacity to recreate the experience in their own imaginations, thus allowing faster and better communication between the two.

For a very short period after the creation of words and abstract thinking, humans began developing quickly as both individuals and as a society. As the danger of predator diminished, our ability to hunt big animals increased, and we developed more efficient ways to build and maintain shelters. The way to the top of the food chain became clear and achievable.

Indeed, this evolution positively impacted our early human ancestors 30,000 years ago. From that moment, it took humans less than 20,000 years to conquer the entire world. Based on recent findings, humans arrived on all the continents by 12,000 years ago, traveling by foot, on tamed animals, or in small boats or carts.

As the saying goes, "The more you understand, the more

you don't know." We can assume this is also applicable to our discussion about the development of language, our capacity to make predictions, and our ability to monitor ourselves and our surroundings. The understanding that we don't control most of the things around us is natural, but a disturbing conclusion if your purpose is to control.

The ability to imagine possible scenarios in our heads helped humans better prepare for actual threats in daily life, but it also brought a host of new concerns and ways to spend free time. Preparing oneself for all possible future disasters, knowing that only one option will eventually happen, is an insane use of time as it is never-ending. Our capacity to expect or hope brought not only a new source of energy to groups and individuals, but brought with it the capacity to be anxious, to be disappointed, and to hold regrets.

Humanity's development of language and abstract thought made us the most sophisticated and complex creatures to ever walk the earth.

We can assume that our modern minds are not so different from the ones who lived 12,000 years ago when it comes to the basic motivation of doing or not doing things. As a group or individuals, the need for security has always been a top priority. An individual that does not know that a specific danger is coming, cannot be concerned about it. while a person that believe that a danger may come cannot avoid being concerned about it. This is the curse of abstract thinking. It is quite natural, that following a short period of practicing such a life, our ancestors arrived to one of our most basic assumption. To promise a safer life an environment for human, the control of the surrounding and its inhabitant is required. As any human need, this idea is healthy as long as it is balanced with counter believes. This need for control, which gave us the motivation needed to conquer the world, has increased regardless of the actual treat existing in our surrounding.

This idea of control for safety still affects almost every aspect of our lives in modern times. Some control makes sense from a societal view—rules and consequences will stop many people from stealing, raping, and killing. We created borders to control the movement of other people and help us feel safe.

In a twisted way, feeling in control of others creates, in humans, a feeling of trust. Let's look at this on a deeper level. If someone is constantly aware that he cannot control his surroundings, it means he cannot predict the future. Living a life in which a person knows he cannot predict future events about himself, his friends, or his surroundings will, without a doubt, cause paranoia and anxiety. It can be assumed, but not proven, that the need for control creates language which, in turn, creates a greater need for control. It is quite common that following the creation of an invention, many new paths and option are created.

It's interesting to think that if the main danger for humans in the last few hundred years has been fellow humans, thus making the source of danger ourselves. To fully understand our complicated existence following the development of language and consciousness, we can look at today's reality. The majority of human concerns today relate to social acceptance, fear of lack of control, and the fear of not meeting one's own personal expectations.

If we want to understand the root cause of our concerns, it boils down to lack of control. Our need for social acceptance is not only based on our need for being part of something bigger, but from our fear of being alone, which makes our ability to predict and control our life harder. This is the main cause for our self-expectation as well. It's quite simple to understand that a person living in isolation doesn't have any self-expectations as he focuses on reality. However, from the moment a person wants to join a group, the demand of the group will be the self-identification of the individual. The first test an individual must pass is explaining to the group who he is and what his intentions are. Such an act will not only require from the individual to explain himself in a way he's never done before, but those ideas become a commitment toward the group immediately. At the end of it, the need of the group to understand who is the person and what are his intentions is a requirement from the side of the group for the purpose of predict the individual's future activity and how it will impact the group in terms of group safety and control over the individual's identity and behavior.

From this moment forward, two different processes will exist in the individual's mind: the need to behave as the group demands and to maintain his own personality as described to the group. Expectations are one of the most abstract and realistic aspect of our life, as it starts in the mind and affect the reality. The "expectation trap" is one of the leading causes of the misery of humans these days as it affects us on many levels:

- Self-expectation
- Expectation from our surroundings.
- The awareness of the surrounding expectation from us.

It's important to mention that without the use of words, the majority of these problems wouldn't exist. That's easy to see. Self-expectation starts in our head, meaning it doesn't reflect the actual reality of our world. We can notice that if the reality lined up with our thoughts, expectations wouldn't exist in the first place. As the thought that we all die in the end is not a matter of expectation, but reality.

The concept of expectation starts from the hope and belief in our head regarding a possible future. These thoughts can only exist by thinking of them with words. The moment in which the thought becomes a problem is when it does not fit the action of the reality. At this moment, an individual will be disappointed, which can bring feelings of impotency, stress, confusion, or depression. The professional term in psychology for such a case is "cognitive dissonance." These negative feelings are understandable, as the individual realizes how minimal control he has over himself and life.

The amusing thing about it is that the definition of the cause of this misery has been made by the person itself from the first place. Let's say I believe I'm a good person and the world is good to good people. If I did something wrong, I could be confused and feel that I don't know myself as good people do not do bad things. From the other side, if bad things happened to me, a feeling the world is a bad place or the possibility that maybe I should be better can arise. This situation will, without any doubt, be troublesome and inflict other aspect of one reality, as when a person loses his confidence in himself, it affects both his personality and his daily life.

The need for leaders to keep individuals under their control requires the ability to predict their future actions and thoughts. Being unable to do so doesn't necessarily make human social groups impossible, but predicting those future actions keeps them all safer and makes grouping easier and the power of the leader safer.

In many peoples' minds, the incapability to explain a phenomenon in words implies that either the phenomenon doesn't currently exist, or that it was impossible to begin with. Their belief that the lack of explanation means something doesn't exist is, at best, misleading them, and secures the impotency of the individual in front of both the individual and its society.

In reality, many concepts in the individual's life don't require an explanation as they are what they are. Even if it is clear that no explanations are required to express the satisfaction of an individual when eating a good chocolate. In many other cases, the incapability of an individual to find words to explain some phenomena could create doubt in the phenomena itself. For example, a random person can live happily all his life without asking himself why, as it's a constant part of his reality. The day a second person asks why the individual is happy, what's causing their happiness, and if they're sure they're happy, the individual will begin to doubt. He'll answer the first question, saying he's happy. The second question will force him, for the first time in his life, to answer in his own words about why he's happy. Because it never occurred to the individual that words are required to explain something he already knows—his own happiness—it will be hard for him to explain it. Now, in case our friend doesn't manage to give good answers to the questions, the person asking the questions, and potentially the individual, might conclude that if no good explanation exists to describe his happiness, maybe he's not really happy. That's absurd, as he felt happiness until just minutes ago. What a disaster for our not any more so happy friend now!

Let's assume that after a short period of reflection, our still happy friend explains why he believes he is happy for the other person. In turn, he'll have a moment of reflection and realize that the explanation isn't good enough, as he shares all of the described traits, but his friend doesn't consider himself happy. Imagine that the second person in questions continues by explaining to our still happy, but confused, friend that he's been around, and real happiness is completely something else, and that to obtain such a quality in the life, work needs to be done. He'll tell our friend that the process to achieve happiness is long and demanding, but that the end result is rewarding. At this moment, the second person comes up with a very peculiar, specific, and abstract way to describe happiness and will follow with the final question: "Are you sure you're happy?" We all know what will be the answer of our previously happy friend.

This is just one example of how words can manipulate reality and control someone's set of beliefs. It's important to mention that different people have strong beliefs about specific things in their life, and some less intense feelings about other things. It's easy to manipulate one set of beliefs just by asking someone to explain those beliefs. The field of sales is professionalized in using such tools for the sake of creating profit. The over use of such a tool can in many cases bring individuals to live a life of confusion and vulnerability.

To fully understand the solution available to our society and individuals for changing the reality we are living in today and building a better future, it's important to recognize were we come from and how we arrived at our current position. As mentioned above, words create ideas, and ideas explain our lives and can be used to manipulate individual minds. Words, language, and communication are both our greatest power and our biggest enemy. They way they're used—not their mere existence—is what makes words, language, and communication so powerful. The tools of language and communication were developed to help humans understand and better control their surroundings. Today, the use of language is used to control us, separate us, and make us doubt our own abilities. By understanding how we got to our current state, we can start to understand the remedy. Solutions for these problems exist and are free for everyone. And the most impressive thing about it? The solution is the exact same set of tools used against us today.

****

Due to the fast changes in both society and communication technology in the last 150 years, humans as a group and as individuals haven't had time to reflect on or react to the drastic changes. We live in a reality in which the values of unity and human life are preached but not practiced, a reality in which we must be right because we fear being wrong, and a reality in which we are willing to ignore the paradoxes that affect us all. We ignore human suffering, lost time, and real emotional connections for the sake of not losing things we never really owned.

How we arrived at this point isn't a mistake or a riddle, but a long process that can be understood if someone holds the right tools for the task. Many psychological studies done in the field of cognitive psychology show that for learning, the process of time passed, reflection, and repetition are key for individuals to develop true understanding of the new information. The ability for humans to think about and reflect on new ideas is the greatest tool developed during our evolution as a species. Abstract thought pushed previous generations to build the world we know today. During the reflection process, two main tools should be available to the individual: a clear understanding of the past and time. The lack of such tools has two possible outcomes: wrong conclusions or no conclusions at all. In the life of the individual in Western society, the constant change and bombardment of people by the media don't give individuals time to reflect and learn. The majority of the population in the West lives life feeling like they don't have time for anything, resulting in less time dedicated to reflection and sleep. This kind of lifestyle is dangerous as it's taking away a main human tool of survival and evolution. When an individual can't reflect on their own existence, they lack self-understanding. Self-understanding is critical for self-image, which helps individuals understand their role in society.

When an individual uses language as described above, they quickly adopt it as their main way of investigating their surroundings. Soon after, this becomes the only tool individuals use to explain their existence first to themselves, and then to the rest of the world.

This way of thinking is very limited. It's impossible to explain what something is without being aware of its opposite or alternative. For example, I can only be a good, beautiful, strong, or successful person if I understand and compare myself to something different, something that competes with those traits. This manner of thinking and categorizing creates fixations and develops vulnerable personalities.

Children understand very quickly that they don't have the verbal capacity to answer questions or meet expectations made by their society. Once children understand that, they search for ideas and words that describe their surroundings. This is a process of trial and error, and children need time to process what works and what doesn't, or time to develop standards of comparison. This self-evaluation becomes impossible if children don't have time and clear examples to develop those standards. Without an understanding of their own capabilities, young people become vulnerable and easily accept standards dictated by outside society. When someone doesn't have the ability to understand himself, he certainly doesn't have the ability to understand the society he lives in. In a society where the majority of individuals don't understand themselves, it's easy for other entities to force philosophies on them, as it gives the individual a sense of understanding and place in society. In general, less the philosophy will require from the individual while presenting a clear self-identity, easier it will be for the individual to accept it on themselves.

Nietzsche declared the death of god over a century ago. Atheism didn't scare Nietzsche, but he feared that people would turn from a blind belief in their God to blindly adopting beliefs prescribed by their governments instead. A standard of living based on a categorization by words is exactly the structure needed for such a change

.

It's All About Education

The fundamental concept of an individual doubting their surroundings is natural and healthy, but can easily be controlled with education. For many years, the governing elite have controlled—or at least monitored—local educational systems. After all, that elite group can only survive if they're accepted by the younger generations, and the place to lay that groundwork is in schools. It's not surprising that some people believe general education is a tool the government uses to promise its long-lasting survival. Government is one of the most sacred tools humans developed over the last few thousand years. It's essential for progress, security, and unity for both small and large groups. Nevertheless, it's extremely important to remember that a government should serve its people, not the other way around. To monitor the government's purpose—as described in the last sentence—we can observe the education system and learn a lot about the local doctrine. If educators begin promoting the government and self-doubt instead of promoting general doubt and criticism, then the government is grasping at self-preservation rather than serving society.

The evolution of Western religions, the creation of mega cities, and globalization have aided in the development of a new use for the tool of doubt. They don't serve as tools to make us question and learn about our environment and freedom, but rather as tools to make us doubt ourselves and who we are. In a world where words are more powerful than actions, and knowledge is used to win arguments under dichotomist philosophical extremes instead of reflecting a capacity to create, individuals learn to doubt themselves and their own experiences rather than their society and government. Changing a population's set of beliefs and values is easier during periods of constant change and individual insecurity. Doubt is an important tool as long as it is used in productive ways for the benefit of the growth of the individual. Education holds the key for acquiring those tools. The importance of a positive and free educational system is crucial in any society and social order. Let's understand why.

Education is the process of learning new information and habits, and all organisms are capable of learning in some capacity. Various education methods include storytelling, discussion, lectures, training, and directed research. This even includes our elders teaching us about our environment, which saves individuals both time and safety. Though trained professionals or elders usually teach, individuals can also practice self-taught education. Self-taught education helps us to understand what is unhealthy or dangerous by trial and observation, and it's a critical part of evolution that's shaped our modern reality.

The idea of education existed long before the creation of our modern education system, and the idea of a general educational standard is a separate topic unrelated to the individual's need for education. Because we are constantly striving to learn more information about our surroundings, education from an external system is naturally accepted as part of the learning process. Our self-understanding is influenced more by our social educations than our self-intrinsic education, as we humans tend to learn from observation and the imitation of our peers. We're all searching for a community to be part of, and it's easy to understand how the behavior of the group we want to join can override all previous education.

Because the educational system of the youngest generation will impact everyone's future, let's concentrate on the general idea of education as a system in our society.

At a young age, the ability of an individual to create their self-image and understand their surroundings is heavily affected by the tools parents give their young children. After the first few years of life, the development of the individual becomes heavily influenced by society, including the individual's peers and the philosophy of their teachers and idols. Fundamentally, an individual's perspective of the world and themselves is mainly built on the perspective developed early in life. Lessons and habits obtained in early age create the foundation for the acceptance of additional information. It explains why it's easier to change a new habit or perspective than an old one. The early education of our children is crucial as it build the foundations for future lessons.

To have deeper conversations about education, we need to establish logical guidelines. First, the willingness and capacity of an individual for any method of education are based on their personality. The personality of the individual is based on their own perspective of themselves and the world around them. Because perspectives are based on the memories of the individual, a person can only be what they remember or have learned consciously or unconsciously. As the creation of memories and their monitoring is the foundation of the creation of our own image and our education, education itself is a process of building new layers on pre-existing foundation and understanding. In other words, memories and education grow like plants; they evolved based on surroundings starting at the roots. It is not a detached process. Deeper the layers are more impact it will have the creation of any new set of believes and behavior.

Now, we must ask two questions regarding the idea of education.

- What are we trying to teach or to learn?
- What measurements are available to show us if the process has been successful?

Those questions need to be clearly established in the beginning of any educational process and need to be consistently revisited by both the teacher and the student. Education is a progressive concept, and if the answers to those questions show negative or insufficient results, the process should change immediately. Without transparency, educational systems become unconstructive and even dangerous, as transparency is an integral part of learning information and questioning the world around us.

To understand the fundamental idea of a healthy education, we must make a distinction between two kinds of education. We'll call the two methods "constructive education" and "depressive education." Constructive education is an education that fundamentally gives an individual the tools needed to acquire information from all sorts, to appreciate and doubt the source of information in hand, and to develop his own conclusions while maintaining the general understanding of what he does not know. Depressive education gives an individual the "absolute" and "unquestionable" truth, rather than tools to learn and question. In other words, depressive education teaches individuals what to think, not how to think.

A depressive education will lead individuals to believe there's only one reality and one truth, and they'll try to apply one logic system to their surroundings. By teaching younger generations how things are and not how things should be done, we're taking away their ability to think, create, and survive. A long period of depressive education will inevitably make society to view different opinions and qualities as negative, while believing that only the majority opinion can be right. This promotes fear of the "other," and leads to separation between people and their neighbors, peers, and society as a whole.

Based on this definition, we can easily observe that today's modern system is mainly depressive. Modern education preaches fear of strange and/or different opinions, materialism, self-concentration, social judgment, and reinforces an existing set of beliefs. It also ignores the growing paradoxes shown by day-to-day reality. We preach knowledge rather than understanding. The modern educational system dictates truths instead of teaching students to question meanings and concepts. It demands blind obedience from students for the reward of social acceptance. The idea that a person should accept things that don't make sense to him from the first place, is a direct consequence of tyrannical education that we've long accepted as part of Western life.

The young generation in the West holds onto a philosophy of fear and terror, creating concern about humanity's ability to create a better future for our children. My personal belief is that an oppressive education controls the Western world, and makes the younger generation feel that the rest of the world is less capable and advanced that Western society. Many individuals raised in the West hold a deep-rooted feeling of fear of other ethnic groups entering and living in those Western countries. This is clearly an attitude taught by depressive education and maintained by ignorance and ego. The depressive educational system of the modern world doesn't supply individuals with the tools they need to manage themselves and their surroundings while understanding "other" culture and ideas. Variations are required for the maintenance of growth and creativity of any society. The fear hold by the western youngsters regarding different religions and cultures is not only demonstrating ignorance regarding this fundamental topic, but is also a holding back the natural evolution of their own society and growth.

An educational system's core mission is to help individuals acquire the tools needed to build a clear self-image and a general understanding of their surroundings. The evolution of an individual from childhood to adulthood can be determined by achieving self-control and an understanding of the individual's ability to change the reality around themselves.

Self-control has been preached by many historical figures as the key for peacefulness and prosperity, and many called it "the middle way." This idea can be found in texts from different points in our history, written or taught by figures like Aristotle, Buddha, Jesus, Muhammed, and more. Because of the middle way's presence across time periods and the world, we could arrive to a conclusion that it is part of an "human universal behavior," as it cross cultures and time.

There's another way to explain this concept. For any material, body or soul, that exists in nature is inseparable from its surroundings. For me to be myself, my boundaries finish at a certain point in space where another entity starts. If an entity is strong enough to stand still in an encounter with an exterior entity, the exterior entity will finish by finding an alternative passage in the moment of encounter. In case the first entity doesn't have the power to stand still, it will be bent by the external entity in the moment or break. A simpler example of this concept is seen when wind or water encounters any object. The wind or water will change its direction if it cannot pass, but it will sweep away anything not strong enough to withstand its power. The same principal is applied to our personality.

The personality of an individual isn't very different. When one personality encounters another—or a society—and doesn't have the power to stand by its own opinion, it will bend and allow the stronger personality to dictate a new perspective. Following such logic, a depressive education, which creates weak personalities, educates the masses to obey and be vulnerable to the tendencies and needs of the system instead of building a strong self-personality that will benefit the individual and the positive evolution of the system itself.

An individual can find peace only when they achieve self-control, rather than when they try to control their surroundings fully and constantly. By controlling themselves, the individual establishes stability and power in their own life. Self-control is necessary not because individuals lack the ability to stop themselves, but because with self-control, they have the freedom to choose or not to choose something. Having control and confidence of oneself inevitably brings peace.

Another trap created by a depressive education is forcing the mind to concentrate on secondary things while ignoring the primary issues. Education concentrated on details ignores the understanding of big-picture ideas. The Pareto Principle—also known as the 80/20 rule, the law of the vital few, and the principle of factor sparsity—states that, for many events, roughly 80% of the effects come from 20% of the causes. Further, it's been found that in many cases, 80% of the work done will take 20% of the time, while the extra 20% of the work will take 80% of the time. This division of work time is based on the assumption of perfect work, in which an imaginary 100% exists in the first place.

At this point, it's important to note an interesting illusion created by Western education that is probably one of the main causes of individual misery. The idea of perfection is imaginary and impractical, as life does not require perfection. Moreover, the 80/20 rule shows why concentrating on perfection is impractical, unproductive, and unsocial outside of the classroom or art domains.

The idea of perfection isn't required in our day-to-day lives, and striving for perfection sucks in many cases all the free time we could have for the growth of other projects or ideas, rather than leaving us to talk and dream about the possibility of having some free time. Moreover, as long as details exist, the importance of the details themselves are, in many cases, irrelevant or a privilege of people with a lot of free time. For example, as long as an individual spoils his/her partner, it's not relevant how they spoil them, as long as some variation of spoiling exists. It's true in the case of manufacturing lines, practical construction, and massive organizations. As long as the general vision and the process is clear, the individuals in the system and the execution of the process is, in many cases, not relevant as long as it exists. We can call it the "law of the big picture."

The law of the big picture is extremely important in any society. In all aspects of society, individuals create groups. It's obvious that each individual will be particular about their own needs and points of view, which is necessary for preserving individuality. On the other hand, as a community or society, fulfilling promises, monitoring security, and making laws regarding specific needs are not practical as it will take too much time and resources. From this point, we can understand that we must establish a general framework and ignore the small details. At this point, the assumption will be that as long as people continue taking care of their needs under the boundaries of the general framework, the government or the system itself won't need to occupy itself with those details. In Western society, where the new generation is educated in a narrow, self-centered view, this philosophy may be hard to grasp. This leads to individuals not understanding their part in the bigger picture and they can't coexist with pluralism and social progress. One of the other negative effects of missing that point is that the belief of an individual in the importance of his wishes and need could weaken the social order and create frustration in the individual mind as his needs are not handled by the group. This is a self-concentrated way to see life that ignores his part in the big picture and doesn't coexist with the concept of pluralism and social progress. A direct effect of depressive education.

Today, the majority of individuals in Western society are preoccupied by the consumption of variations of the same products and lack free time. The unimportance of detail is extremely important for the sake of liberation from the tyranny of the mind.

The longer an individual concentrate on the importance of details, the harder it is for them to accept the idea of the unimportance of details, as they are but a poor tool used by humans to express a general phenomenon. Words always have a tone, but a tone doesn't always require words. Words and products will pass and be forgotten, but the essence of their usage will stay for eternity. Every product reflects a specific idea, and specifics ideas can be reflected in many products. Tone and ideas develop with time, while time kills words, products, and even human beings. A depressive education teaches individuals to concentrate on the details while creating a reality in which a lack of control and understanding. From the other side, a constructive education gives individuals the tools needed to ignore the details as long as they exist and concentrates on the general movement or the ideas behind it.

The more materialism grows, the farther we'll move away from the love, peace, and respect we had for ourselves and our surroundings. The more we're educated by a depressive system, the harder it will be for individuals to think for themselves. A human who doesn't possess the tools needed to understand themselves and accept their society will find it hard to feel their own existence, as they're taught that without the ability to attach words or materials to an entity, that entity does not exist.

****

The reality we live in is twisted and unconstructive, and we can see it all around the world. Budgets for public education are low at best, and survives solely based on teachers' willingness to dedicate their lives to the creation of a better educational system. This willingness is a sacrifice as it comes at the price of low wages—even poverty—while bankers and bureaucrats live lavish lifestyles, pursuing their own self-interests and personal profit. Researchers around the world have shown that the status and respect for educators has dropped in the eyes of both parents and students in the last 30 years. Additionally, the educational plans and materials chosen for public schools are influenced not by the values of progress and prosperity of the community itself, but by the belief of building individuals that will fit the needs of the government in the future.

As we acquired the ability to share knowledge globally and unite humanity as one, education that doesn't promote the good of humanity and nature itself is ignorant and cannot be supported by any logic. The suffering of African peoples and the destruction of their land for the sake of maintaining Western comfort doesn't promote long-term progress in either location, and is a paradox hidden by an education of fear, ignorance, and separation. We need an educational system that creates a foundation for peace, prosperity, and productivity for our species as whole. The period of separation was a matter of ignorance and can no longer exist as we have transformed into a global society.

Alternative forms are education are varied and positive. By itself, a constructive education isn't a specific way of teaching, but a thought process that dictates the future of our children and the world. Education is the essence of knowledge, which is the foundation of progress and unity. It's not a matter of what is right or wrong from a personal perspective, but what is constructive or destructive for society. The foundation of the new educational system should be a system of tolerance for what we do not understand based on peacefulness and awareness. We owe it to our children and to ourselves to leave the world a better place than how we found it. Movements start based on understanding between individuals, which creates groups and then nations.

Equality and Freedom

The concepts of equality and freedom are in the thoughts of the individual more than ever in Western society. The use of those terms without knowing their history is dangerous and deceiving to both society and individuals. The combination of the terms freedom and equality as referred to today is both new and contradictory. For many years, freedom has been a tool used by government to terrorize its citizens and engage in wars against other countries and minority groups. Many examples exist for this behavior. The majority of the wars waged by Western societies have been launched under two main explanations: to free the foreign population from a local injustice or the protection of the nation against a potential threat to the current freedom of its citizens. The Nazis saw Jews as a threat, and the wars in Afghanistan and Iraq were launched under both of the explanations. The Christian crusades, the current war in the Middle East, and the Cold War are but a few examples out of the history of Western wars.

A war launched based on the philosophy of preserving the equality freedom of a certain nation is a paradox. To understand how terms that occupied generations of intellectuals became tools of control, we should start by separating the two concepts and examining their evolution as separate entities.

Equality

Before discussing these topics, it's important that we agree on a few guidelines. If we are all good at different things, as one is better than the other in music or mathematics and vice versa, then it's fair to say we are not equal in our physical and mental capacities. Humans has been gifted with a variety of different activities in which individuals achieve different results. The idea that we're all born as humans is a simplistic way to group us for the purpose of unification. Unification is positive, but it does not make us equal. We can say that all mammals are born the same way, but does this make us equal to a cow or a dog? In the reality of life, individuals are born with different capacities that make them a unique person. We are indeed closer to true equality than at any other point in human history, but believing that we currently live in an equal world or society is unrealistic.

Equality, which is a broad concept, is a human creation that stems from our ability for conceptual ideas and words. No terms similar to the word equality can be found unrelated to human activities. In the ancient period, the use of political equality was a term which gave to a small amount of people, under certain standards, the same rights to practice politics while still enslaving another part of the population. Such a use of the term of equality was valid and practiced in the time of Aristotle, and it reappeared as a fundamental idea in England in the 13th century and then during the creation of the United States. Following different forms of government in the history and political movement, we see different scenarios in which the idea of equality has been used. For example, Christian thinkers discuss individuals as equal in front of God. It's important to understand at this point that throughout human history, equality hasn't been used as an abstract term for a general equality by governments, religions, or other groups, as it contradicts the foundation of those systems. The concept of equality contradicts the concentration of power. Specifically, in our days the idea of equality contradicts in many aspects the idea of capitalism. This will be discussed in the following chapter.

So, what is equality all about? One of the ways to approach this subject is to look at equality as a variety of social, political, and economic activities available to all individuals regardless of their gender, religion, origin, or social class. As practiced until today, equality can refer to rights in front of the law, equality of opportunity, equal political rights, and so on. Referring to equality without specifying the type of equality, or by using it as a general term, becomes a tool of mass manipulation. Society's elite have a responsibility to monitor the population's general perceptions of the world, making sure the masses understand terms used in society. If the population doesn't understand the values they're fighting for, it will weaken the society as a whole.

Looking at the use of the term equality throughout history, only recently has it been used as a general social and economic philosophy. For example, the equality of the Frenchmen during the French Revolution doesn't refer to the equality of the French to the Germans or any other population. At the time of its founding, the equality of opportunity in the United States referred to white, land-owning, American men and their political rights. Now, with globalization on its way, the concept of equality refers to the tyranny of Western population first and then the rest of the world's populations.

It's also important to mention that since the original mention of the word, the equality of the elite existed only thanks to the enslavement of the others. This is a trend that continued throughout history. Also in our days, there's equality in Western civilization thanks to the enslavement of Eastern and African populations in ways of production, manufacturing, mining, and importation of goods. Only masters need slaves, never the opposite. Deeper understanding of this notion of equality will bring you, the intellectual reader, to the conclusion that equality by itself has been invented by elite groups for the sake of gaining cooperation of and separation from the rest of society.

Looking back and understanding the use of the term of equality isn't all negative. It teaches us about our evolution, past societies, and ourselves. We're the first generation with access to the endless information available about our evolution. We'll look more at the big evolutional steps from the last 300 years in Chapter 3, but we may be on the verge of creating a reality in which, for the first time in history, equality can truly be referred to as a broad, global concept. The purpose of those writings is to support in at least one way such a process.

Equality can be viewed two different ways based on what it requires from its subjects. A philosophy claiming that equality doesn't require anything from the individual is problematic, as then it's just an abstract idea. If an individual possesses an abstract thing that they never need to act on, they'll only feel its absence when it's taken from them. At this point, as the individual never did anything to acquire it in the first place, or never practiced it, they'll miss the tools needed to restore it if lost. Some may claim that because the person didn't do anything to acquire this equality, never used it, and doesn't have the tools to get it back, then that individual never actually had equality. Following that logical path, we can conclude that a philosophically abstract equality never truly exists for individuals.

So, how can we use the concept of equality? Let's continue to follow our logic. For an individual to actually acquire the practice of equality, they'll have to gain those rights by taking action. This philosophy is straight forward. If an individual wants equal political rights, they'll be required to contribute to society politically. If an individual would like to have equality as a citizen, they must be an active part of their community. In this sort of equality, there must be a clear separation between what's required, how to monitor the system, and the actual equal traits. In such a system, it's important to maintain equal opportunities, which allow any person the opportunity to practice their rights to take part. It can be predicted that in such a system, the majority of the population will prefer not to practice part of the necessities to acquire a full and complete equality, as it'll require too much time and energy. The individual's free choice not to practice their rights and obtain true equality doesn't affect the same opportunities for others. As long as the entire population has the opportunity to practice their duties and earn their rights, that society will achieve a system of a healthy, relative equality.

In the late 20th century, we began a conversation about equal human rights, which brought forward an idealistic set of human rights. This idealistic set, while positive and beautiful, is also deceptive. Western society determined what constitutes equal human rights, and it's so utopian that it can't be practice or enforced in our society. If such a world was possible, decent people would surely be happy to practice it. But as long as we fail to create and protect relative equality in our own societies, we should leave other populations to handle themselves. It's impossible for a person to teach without learning first, and a society that hasn't learned or established such a system certainly can't preach one to other nations.

The pursuit of the idea of equality is positive, but it

requires practicality. The pursue after abstract and unachievable concept is unhealthy for a society and dangerous for its neighbors. As we become more aware of the world, we become more aware of its misery. It is easier to try to correct other rather than facing one own problems. When approaching subjects that are so general and abstractive, it is important to understand that time is required for creating a real change. In those cases, it is not the result that matter, but the process, as it affects actual lives and shape societies. Words creates concepts, that creates actions, that creates changes. The misconception of the concept of equality is dangerous. A wrong definition of the terms can create more misery to entire populations than to improve any current state.

Freedom

Freedom is another interesting subject that's been problematic during human history. By examining history, we can see that under different government systems, the preservation of freedom had a direct correlation with the survival of the elite, the destruction of the rest of the population, and the creation of slavery under each system.

It's important to note that the concept of general freedom has never been taken or considered seriously in any political party, as the concept is paradoxical to the foundation of any society. The freedom of numerous individuals in a limited space, by its own definition, creates the lack of freedom of another, as they are two sides of the same coin. It is true to say that the abstract definition of freedom doesn't create such limitations. For example, the Oxford dictionary defines freedom as "the power or right to act, speak, or think as one wants." Practically, from the moment more than one individual coexist in a system, the freedom of the other will inevitably limit the freedom of the first. For example, the existence of the first in a limited space will inevitably limit the freedom to move of another as he is occupying a certain space. The sound the first makes limits, in many cases, the freedom of another person to speak. For more information about all of the above points, read *On Politics* by Alan Rayn or any other historical book on the subject.

It's strange to observe that this knowledge doesn't reflect the opinion and understanding of freedom by the masses of those historical periods. The conclusions of those writings are relevant to the concept of freedom as a general term that never existed in humanity and not as a global term in practice. In Western social philosophy, in which waste creation is ignored and progress is humanity's main purpose, the freedom of one group or individual requires the denial of the same freedom to another group/person. Another paradox of freedom is that to be accepted by a society, an individual will have to give away the natural state of freedom we're all born into. Western readers born into this societal structure may find this idea hard to grasp. This doesn't make the point less relevant. This point is not always negative, as diminishing one freedom brings one additional security.

As long as freedom is chained to the idea that an individual must compromise their freedom or another person's freedom, this paradox will always exist.

Logically, the term freedom can be used regarding specific domains, as a person can have freedoms in specific domains. An individual can have the freedom to walk in the street of their town, the freedom of choosing their own meals, and the freedom to buy whatever they want.

"Real freedom" is a term coined by the political philosopher and economist Philippe Van Parijs. It expands upon notions of negative freedom by incorporating not simply institutional or other constraints on a person's choice, but also the requirements of physical reality, resources, and personal capacity.

According to Van Parjis, to have real freedom, an individual must:

1. Not be prevented from acting on their will (i.e. They must have traditional negative freedom); and

2. Possess the resources or capacities to actually carry out their will.

Under this concept, a moral agent could be negatively free to take a holiday in Miami, because no one is forcing them not to (condition 1 is met). But, they're not really free to do so because they cannot afford the flight (condition 2 is not met). Similarly, someone could be negatively free to swim across the English Channel, but not really free because they aren't a good enough swimmer and would fail.

Real freedom, then, is a matter of degree. One is more or less really free, not just either free or not, and no one has complete real freedom—no one is really free to teleport to Mars, for instance. To learn more about this subject, search Real Freedom on Wikipedia.

Freedom should be promoted. More freedom exists today than it ever did in human history. Wars and massacres in the name of freedom are a negative use of the concept used to manipulate and serve self-interest groups. It's our responsibility to monitor it and make sure it is well used.

***

The idea of freedom and equality as a combined concept in Western society is a paradox, as neither of the terms makes sense by itself as a practical general term. The equality of an individual in his society contradicts the fundamental idea of capitalism and the hierarchical arrangement of human societies. The idea of freedom is impossible in a society that requires different social classes and enslavement for the sake of its existence, while creating waste and pollution for the sake of the pursuing profit by the elite.

It's fascinating to see that in the Western world, we acquire our equality and freedom as citizens by not coming into contact with law enforcement or government agents. Let's take a moment to make it clearer. If only at the moment a citizen loses his freedom or rights, he at the same very moment discovers the freedom he lost, would it be possible to say he never had it from the first place? Could we say the government just let him live with such an illusion? Does a prisoner in jail who never thought about leaving really feel like he wasn't free to leave? A long period of ruling such a society can make individuals paranoid and passive, as the fear of losing what you have is undoubtedly a complex and disturbing situation.

This misconception regarding those terms is just an example of the importance of using the right abstractive terms and the danger of using words we do not fully understand. As the majority of our decision-making and self-image start and develop in our heads, the importance of the right educational system that will give the populous the right tools to use and understand what terms to use is more important than ever. We have the power to shape our future together. A clear and achievable goal needs to be determined for the success of such a process. A well-educated society holding the right terms and a good understanding of the reality, without any doubts is a good starting point.

45

Chapter 2:

Economy and politics

Introduction to the 21st Century

The economic and political structure of the world as we know it today has evolved into a world in which nations are inseparable one from another thanks to the net of what we call "the global market" or "globalization." Local markets cannot supply the majority of products consumed without importing from other countries. In many cases, goods manufactured in a specific country cannot maintain local production without importing natural resources or exporting large quantities. Political agendas and actions are influenced by other countries, and the majority of manufacturers countries work to maintain profitability, which is based on exporting goods.

The idea of the evolution of the net called "globalization," isn't new. Empires have tried to conquer the world for millennia. But, the evolution of globalization in the last 300 years has brought a new reality in which we are, for the first time, close to achieving such an objective. The capacity of humans to create a global network is directly and inseparably connected to the rise of imperialism, the industrial revolution, the rise of capitalism, and the current technological revolution. This new system has brought many positive upgrades to humanity and some negative ones.

It's important to mention that in a natural evolutionary process, trial and error is required. Such a process is natural and positive, bringing some negative trials on the ways. The capacity of a population to evolve positively is, in many cases, connected directly to the capacity of the population to keep the positive results and dump the negative ones. Our ability to connect globally, to trade freely with the rest of the world, and to share knowledge instantly are, without any doubt, positive aspects of human evolution. From the other side, the enslavement and impoverishment of the majority of Earth's population, national debts, political structures allowing concentration of power, and the promotion of self-interest are all negative parts of our evolution.

The majority of the world's population knows that we evolved to live and operate in such a structure. Nevertheless, only a select group truly understand this concept and its consequences. The economic global market and its structure are a direct evolution of the progress of Western society and its domination over the globe in the last 500 years. Looking at the evolution of our economy, the process that brought us to today's reality began in Europe around the 17th century. During this period, the rise of imperialism created the need for local governments to raise more funds to pursue world domination and power. Looking back at history, it's easy to understand how the need for mass expansion brought a new need for more funds and investment. As the discovery of new lands and cultures came with the discovery of its natural resources, it's not surprising that individuals were willing to invest in conquered territories. Those tools of profit and conquer created the tools necessary for the Western empire to spread and conquer the world as we know it today.

Looking at the evolution of humanity, a period of a few hundred years is short compared to the time we've existed. Nevertheless, the global, social, and psychological changes in that period are incomparable in their effects to any prior period in history. The Western empire started to massively evolve during the 17th century. This period of discovering and conquering the globe arrived at its peak in the mid-20th century. In those few hundred years, the Western empires controlled more than 50% of Earth known to humanity, including big parts or all of Africa, the Americas, Australia, and Asia. The discovery of new lands came with new knowledge, access to new cultures, resources, and new food. Looking at the menu of European societies, it's quite amazing to discover that the majority of the basic nutrition of its people don't originate in Europe. Potatoes, rice, coffee, sugar, tobacco, and silk are only a few examples of basic commodities Europeans took from other cultures.

Unfortunately, as imperialism was pursued based on philosophies of racism, violence, and supremacy, one of the most visible effects of the arrival of the European empire to new territories was the mass murder of local populations, the exploitation of natural resources, and the re-culturisation of the surviving population based on European values and needs.

As the world evolved, the Western empire's physical control over the rest of the world weakened, forcing the West to liberate the majority of it colonies between 1935 and 1970. It's important to mention that, in many cases, the liberation was only physical, as the Western empire kept local political power to maintain the exploitation system built up over decades. The enslavement and extraction system by the West in South America and Africa in 2017 is proof of the control held even after fall of the imperialism.

Due to the long and aggressive control by the West over the rest of the world, the foundational philosophy, local culture, progress made in those markets, and the values held in the liberated countries has allowed the West to control these lands from distance. As the evolution of our kind has evolved this way, the best way to understand the modern world is done by following the growth and evolution of Western society and its domination on the economic world. From this point of view, the rest of the global events are the reaction of the rest of the world's population to the growth and changes brought and enforced by the West during the last 500 years.

At first, the world we live in today looks complicated and detached from the individual living in it. The governments of the world are suffocating under the national debt concept pushed by the rise of capitalism and the overuse of politics. The enslavement of the people of Africa and Asia that used to be explained to the Western population as a need for European enrichment, doesn't reflect the modern reality of Western individuals as they are becoming poorer and more fragile while a small community of individuals has taken control over the political and governmental process of evolution for the sake of promoting their wealth and personal self-interest.

As we'll see in this chapter, this system isn't hard to understand if addressed subject by subject. It indeed requires patience and effort, as we'll need to break a few fundamental ideas rooted in our education. But, the need to see the reality as it is— and not how we would like it to be—is an essential process to understand the modern world. Magnificent tools have been developed for the promotion of the wellbeing of humans and the planet. The consciousness of individuals achieved these days has created many movements concentrating on creating a better world. The global communication network is part of this solution. From the other side, we'll see old habits like the concentration of power, the enslavement of another for profit, and the manipulation of the masses to maintain power are all part of behaviors rooted in our social system that don't promote the wellbeing of humanity. We'll better understand where those habits come from and what we're actually aiming to achieve. Those topics are fundamental as they affect every aspect of our life. If we are striving to create a better future for our families and children, those topics needs to be challenged and understood.

The belief that things are as they are because it's the best solution out of bad options is mediocre and dangerous. As discussed in the previous chapter, the majority of problems existing in 2017 are created by humans. The enrichment of the few in power, the enslavement and impoverishment of the rest of the population, the unnecessary killing of animals for the sake of the creation of waste, the destruction of nature, and the violent way to terrorize our mind are not a necessity, but a well-built system. Many organizations exist today fighting for specific causes. The anti-corruption organizations, bio and natural awareness organizations, vegetarian movements, global warming organizations, human rights, and peace organization are all fighting the same fight. As we will see, all those subjects are connected and can be boiled down to how we govern ourselves and maintain our economy. Following the reading of this book, I hope and believe that a new door will be opened. As the separation of people and concepts are just tools held by the tyrannical government to weaken the population and maintain profit at the cost of our peace and freedom.

Ideas about Governments and Politics

Government is an administrative and bureaucratic organization that needs to be evaluated as such. Government actions should be clear and transparent to its citizens. Government's role is to promote the happiness and peacefulness of its citizens while encouraging intellectual and social growth. Governments are created for the sake of the prosperity of society as a whole, and any government that has acted differently in the past has been classified as tyrannical and has been destroyed by natural political movements. After all, citizens now give governments their power, and it would be absurd for individuals to live under a government not fulfilling its duties. Moreover, the purpose of a society is to encourage and create free time and prosperity of its citizens. Nevertheless, the elite governing group growing rich on the success of its citizens is the common reality of most societies, organizations, and structures known to us in the Western world.

When approaching the subject of politics and government, it's important to make a distinction between the two. Understanding the differences between the two, and their application in a governance system, isn't something well-known and understood by many. The lack of understanding by the population that the idea of politics and government can and should be separated, is one of the main reasons why nations and the global economic network is problematic those days.

Let's take the time to understand why. From the moment a population grows to a certain size, the creation of a manager or supervisor role is recommended for that population's efficiency and its success. The bigger the population, the less the management job will be connected to the actual job of its working teams. As seen in many organizations, management is a profession by itself. This profession is evaluated based on the capacity of the management to choose the right people for the actual tasks, articulating clear objectives, and monitoring the work process. Management is a necessity in any big organization as many fields need to be covered and there must be cooperation amongst employees. To make it simple, due to the cooperation needed and the number of communal areas, creating a role that's in charge of operations and the common good leads to improved functionality for employees, the system, and its workers. Government's job isn't very different from a big company or an airport. It needs to manage and handle a lot of practical jobs, bureaucratic jobs, marketing jobs, and so on. The more a population grows, the bigger the need for the managing party to maintain its efficiency. It is important to mentioned, that also organization that do not pursue profit, requires a management team for its efficiency.

In Chapter 3, we'll evolve the ideas related to the positive and negative aspects of expanding nations and mega nations and the possible implication regarding the government. At this point of our reading, we'll instead concentrate on understanding the fundamental role of a government, what it should not be, and which kind of governments currently lead us. For now, an important conclusion is that as long a certain degree of efficiency and a certain population level exists, the creation of a managing party is both healthy and required. Following the evolution of the Western world to administer itself under a democratic government structure, the main job of a governing party should be a managerial, bureaucratic, and administrative institution that promotes the safety and well-being of its citizens under the philosophy presented during election time.

Politics, on the other hand, is completely a different subject. The definition of politics on Wikipedia is as follows:

"Politics (from Greek: Politiká: Politika, definition "affairs of the cities") is the process of making decisions applying to all members of each group. More narrowly, it refers to achieving and exercising positions of governance — organized control over a human community, particularly a state. Furthermore, politics is the study or practice of the distribution of power and resources within a given community as well as the interrelationship between communities. A variety of methods are deployed in politics, which include promoting or forcing one's own political views among people, negotiation with other political subjects, making laws, and exercising force, including warfare against adversaries. Politics are exercised on a wide range of social levels, from clans and tribes of traditional societies, through modern local governments, companies and institutions up to sovereign states, to the international level. It is very often said that politics is about power. A political system is a framework which defines acceptable political methods within a given society."

Based on this definition, politics is mainly related to

philosophy and sociology, often time used by force and trickery for self-interest. As the field of politics is mainly philosophical and social, many times it's not the ideas that are right or wrong, but the practical implication determines whether it will be right or wrong. Without a doubt, managing a state is better done when backed by research and a clear philosophical vision. A clear vision, mission, and understanding of the available tools are necessary for the creation of a good managing party to start with. From the other side, all of those things can be achieved without overusing political tools. The dangerous aspect of politics is that without a clear vision and a practical back-up, this field quickly devolves into trickery, bribery, manipulation, and crime. Today's politics have become another name for the pursuit of power and the government as a whole. The creation of a system in which governments and politics are inseparable is one of the reasons the population is reluctant to seriously address those fields. As politics are taking over the governments, the use of violence has become the main tool used by the government itself.

The use of violence by the government against its own citizens is wrong and, in many cases, a twisted way for a government to use its power. It's true to say that in the modern world, it can look like violence is the only way governments keep society in order. Alas, government violence should be a last resort solution and not a daily philosophy to maintain power. The creation of jail houses, police fortresses, and armed forces made for the sake of protecting the citizens from themselves--rather than an outside threat—is a manipulated explanation of reality. In truth, the government builds those systems to keep itself safe from the population. After a few decades of such violent management, the majority of the world sees the concept of government as distant, violent, and hostile.

Governments should use political tools to do a better job, and let's not forget that the government's job is promoting the well-being of its citizens. Unfortunately, political tools are often used by the self-interested elite who hide behind empty philosophies. Without a doubt, politics is an important tool, but not a necessity to maintain neither a country, state, or company.

A simple parameter can immediately detect the overuse of politics: If the state's economy rises and technology improves, life—including income and free time—should improve for the masses. If that's true, but the masses do not see the benefits of income and free time, then the real beneficiaries of the new reality are the elite manipulating the population with the tools of politics. In such a case, it's safe to say that politics is occupying the government and not the opposite. Moreover, the lack created in the lives of the masses creates a loop which supports the self-interest of the politicians in power. A system in which an individual doesn't have resources to enjoy their free time leads to a fear of losing what individuals don't have. Such a reality creates a deep feeling of loneliness, which creates the mental ignorance needed for a tyrannical government to hold control without the threat of individuals fighting back.

As a conclusion, it's important to understand that the governing parties of our democratic societies should be in power for the sake of benefiting the wellbeing and prosperity of their citizens. The need for an administrative, managing party is necessary as the population of the cities and countries are growing. From the other side, the use of violence, manipulation, and the pursue of self-interest are contradictory the fundamental ideas of a democratic governing country, as they are all tools used by tyrants and monarchs. Politics, as a main way of operating a democratic government, is a paradoxical reality, as the use of violence against the society, the use of power for serving self-interests, and the impoverishment of the population are contradicting the need for a government in the first place. In many peoples' minds, government *IS* politics. We accept the idea that government makes a profit, and the idea that the good of the country outweighs the needs of the individual is deeply rooted in people's minds. As we will see later in this reading, all of those thoughts are habits that managed to stay in our societies after millennia of monarchy and tyranny. If done correctly, the creation of a democratic government is a positive evolution that empowers the people, as it creates a decentralized well monitored organization.

From the other side, calling a government democracy just because it's not a monarchy is a misconception of vocabulary that doesn't benefit society as it should. Looking at Western societies, we can see that people have a general idea of what a true democracy should be while still knowing that they're far from living in one. Governments abusing the tools of violence, politics, and fear are serving self-interest at best, and are a different type of ruler than democracy. The separation of those tools from our ruling parties is one of the most important steps toward a reality in which the government will start benefiting its citizens.

The creation of such a government is new, as is the idea of democracy. Looking at European history, the creation of a real democratic system is new, dating back less than 200 years. In the majority of European countries, the liberation from a monarch and tyrant was only completed in the 20th century. From the other side, as we are working on evolving new societies based on new ideals, it's important to understand what to keep from our old ruling systems and what to abandon. But, how can we manage to separate the positive and negative aspects of our ruling system? As we're in the middle of this evolution, a clear structure isn't available. Maybe management is as dynamic as life and cannot work based on a fixed structure. From the other side, by laying down the fundamental ideology of how to create a democratic government, the practical system will emerge by itself.

The Professional Governing Model

The creation of a government to lead its citizens has existed for as long as humans have formed societies. Because of this, it's inevitable to conclude that a leading party governing a population is the natural way of arranging a society. We can assume that the existence of government has been created out of the population's need, and has maintained its role of supporting society regardless of time or location. It's also noticeable that specific types of people have engaged in governing roles over time. Such tendency is natural and healthy; different people have different strengths and occupations. Some individuals are better than their peers at making tough decisions, and some people have more passion for leadership than others.

Most of the individuals in Western society will allow any kind of government to exist as long as the governing elite don't require drastic changes in the day-to-day activities of its citizens, and as long as the citizens have a general feeling of fairness and peacefulness in society. This point is very important. These days, a lot of people have strong opinions regarding both local and global politics and world affairs. From the other side, those opinions are formed more for the sake of creating daily conversation, and in most of the cases, don't evolve into actions. The idea that specific kinds of people are made for politics is as trivial as the idea that specific kinds of people should be doctors. It's neither good nor bad, just a reflection of how things are.

As understood by many writers and leaders throughout history, any organization requires a group of individuals equipped with the knowledge and capacity to lead. There have long been conversations about the need for professional people in the right position. The idea that some of us are better at governing doesn't contradict any democratic ideas, but promotes a healthy society monitored by many. An individual working in their own store may not be qualified to or have the tools to understand the intricacies of economics, healthcare, and defense, but *can* understand which policies will have positive or negative effects on their life. Admitting that our individual capacities are limited and understanding what we are not capable of doing is fundamental to a healthy system. For a healthy system to function, there must be clear definitions of roles and responsibilities across many sectors, and it's important for individuals to know which role they best fit.

Knowing that specific people should concentrate on their strengths and let other professionals handle their own fields is ideal for a healthy society. It's utopian thinking that all citizens are not only constantly equal in status, but always equal in their participation in society. This thinking contradicts the need for government and society. As we agree that we should let professionals make decisions in their own fields, it would be absurd to task unequipped masses with making both day-to-day decisions and complex choices for society and government, From the other side, the decision makers cannot go unchecked. For a governmental system to work for the benefit of its population, the professionalism of the decision making has to be checked and evaluated by the masses, *not* the decision maker itself.

Decision making is a responsibility to be taken by individuals. One of the natural outcomes of making decisions is sometimes making the wrong one. On a national scale, the outcome of a good decision may be negative from the point of view of an unprofessional person who doesn't understand the cause and effect of the decision. Without a doubt, good decisions can have bad outcomes, though that doesn't make that decision a bad one in the big picture. As decision making is a matter of calculating and understanding the stream of events and potential consequences, the unprofessional masses cannot judge a decision. As true as it is, the incapability of the masses to judge the decision-making process doesn't imply that it's not possible for them to understand its consequences. A system built on the evaluation of decisions of the governing group and not the professionalism of its work will be open to manipulation of the masses by powerful group of self-interest.

It's fascinating to observe that most of the citizens of any city in history prefer passing their time doing what they like and are good at. Recent research in cognitive psychology supports this, and found that the energy required from an individual when involved in matters behind the spectrum and occupation of an individual—such as politics and economy—require enormous amounts of time and energy that could be better spent elsewhere. From a mathematical perspective, a person who spends their time constantly handling an occupation not well known and controlled will require all of their available cognitive power. A long period of such a behavior will create an overwork of the system that prevents specialization in a specific field. Such energy loss complicates the life of the individual and is unnecessary for maintaining their happiness. This idea had been part of common logic in the past, but seems to be lost on our generation.

The new philosophical approach of the individual in Western society, which not only believes in the need of a self-opinion, but the need for a self-opinion which is in line with their peers' perception is one of the causes for such a cognitive overload. This is anti-democratic and contradictory to the concept of pluralism, which is fundamental to maintaining a free and healthy population. The need for the right, educated people in government who will constantly be valued for their practical achievement, and the need for a population of individuals able to recognize themselves and understand the system they are living in, is important for the sake of the future of the democratic and political system we are living in. It's also important for individuals to feel they have control and understand the consequences of their actions for the sake of maintaining a healthy government.

Many paradoxes regarding the beliefs of the masses—including their understanding of society and reality—exist in today's society. These paradoxes are a mental structure created by the ruling elite and the media to maintain the tyranny of profit and self-interest. The idea that people should concentrate on themselves and desire wealth is one of the biggest social paradoxes. We will see in this chapter how the greed of profit and the self-concentration concepts are anti-social and anti-democratic.

Another paradoxical example is the technological progress we're all so proud to march to. The Western world strives to invent machines to do tasks for us to free up our time, but in reality, these advances are tools used to impoverish the masses and grow unemployment. It's true that theoretically, we have the capacity to achieve a better reality through technology, but as long as the government allows the existence of the political elite we know today, we'll continue to live far away from such a reality. Moreover, the banks, which have supposedly been created to support the market and keep the population's money safe, control the government and create both private and national debt. Debts hunting us on a daily basis.

The consequences of operating a government controlled by politics affects both the organization itself and its citizens. As a government is an administrative and a management organization, there needs to be a clear philosophy that describes and maintains its role. As concluded above, the government's main purpose is to promote the wellbeing of its citizens and the prosperity of the country. it's important that the foundation of the government be kept in this order. In most of cases, the two will support each other as the country is made up of its citizens. Such a philosophy is clear and easy to evaluate. Maintaining such a clear philosophy allows the citizens to have an understandable parameter to judge its government. In such an organization, as long as politics are used as a tool based on the clear principle described above, the tool can be healthy and positive for society.

The use of politics in a system that doesn't have or

maintain a clear philosophy is dangerous, as the system is weak and can be easily affected by manipulation. As politics is the capacity of exercising positions of governance and achieving organized control over a human community, the best politician may not be the best person to operate a government. In many cases, people who possess a talent for politics do not possess the necessary skills to operate a large organization. Many times, good politicians require good social skills, or the ability to manipulate situations and hold the philosophy of a worrier. From the other side, the head of a big organization requires different qualities such as the ability to operate under pressure, meet goals, and delegate decision making. In many cases, the qualities of a good manager are contradictory or parallel to the qualities of a politician. Unfortunately, the way things are done today, the politician is more probable to win election than the good, skilled person.

The control of politics on governments promises that the personal philosophy of the leader of the hour will drastically affect the decision making and evolution of the entire government and its citizens. A long period of ruling by a self-interested government will inevitably change the social structure and the values of the individuals in the country. This point is important as it makes it easier to understand how a nonprofit organization like a government manages to get involved in profit and surplus.

Claims that we require good politicians in power comes from the ancient way we governed ourselves. In the last 500 years, a new philosophy involving the creation of profit by investment has been promoted in Western culture. In times of kings and empires, the capacity to hold the ruling position required a skillful politician. After all, it was a period of individual rulers threatened by their closest people for the position itself. In many cases, the leader's ability to survive was based on his capacity to react simultaneously aggressively and wisely. History if full of good examples that can help us understand why, evolutionarily speaking, leaders of the past had to be good politicians.

The creation of a democratic social system has led to a new reality in which we can separate politics from government. Leaders don't need to manipulate populations to maintain power if said power is maintained by a general standard. The requirements demanded of a governor don't require the use of politics to get or maintain that position. By creating a healthy, democratic governing system that prescribes clear goals and is evaluated by its ability to achieve them, leaders won't need manipulation or political plots. A simple straight forward structure can be built. In this structure, the population should vote separately for each ministry post. The candidates have to show practical experience in the field and should promote a clear plan of action if chosen. As such, a system constructed on simple information has no need for politics which will drastically diminish the budget needed in elections. The professional structure will promise effective execution that can be monitored with the time. Such a structure is just an example for an alternative way of managing a government. Many other options exist. The important point is that no politics are required in election if the model is based on the professionality of the candidate and not their capacity to engage in politics.

Unfortunately, in Western societies, political skill is required and used to get elected rather than for improving the state of the people. The elite and the self-interested opportunists manage modern politics. As the separation between the need for politics and government wasn't clear at the creation of our modern system, the elite's ability to manipulate the government by politics brought nations to operate based on self-interested philosophies and not the common good.

Making such a change can seem complicated from our current perspective. Any change requires effort, and any effort is worth spending if the desired results are achieved. Humanity is standing at a crossroads. Focusing on minute details and things that might go wrong are paranoias that shouldn't occupy a living organization as it will continue to evolve with or without our willingness to join that evolution. The way we govern ourselves affects every aspect of our lives and surroundings. Ideological principle should guide us, not momentary opinion. Based on the numerous organizations fighting to make a better world in 2017, the number of professionals available for managing our countries and world exists; we just need to unite them and give them the possibility to work. The separation of politics from government is crucial. Operating our government without such a separation will maintain the principles of the old monarchies and tyrannies.

Early Capitalism and Our Monetary System

To better understand the life we live today, we need to understand the concept of capitalism, its aggressive entry into the governing system, and its outcome. Capitalism, as it's known today, has grown and evolved following the Industrial Revolution thanks to the increase in manufacturing capacity and the slave trade. The explanation and categorization of the idea and practice of capitalism as utopian or a far-right ideology comes from ignorance of our reality. Capitalism is the fundamental way we've been running things for at least 50 years. We can see it everywhere, from our economic structure, investment in research, and our individual dreams. The better we will understand this and accept it, the easier it will be for us to find a solution.

As we'll see, capitalism has come to affect every aspect of our lives, from the workplace to the employment structure to the dreams of the individuals in society. By understanding the idea of capitalism, we'll see how the need for globalization and the impoverishment of the many are just the outcomes of a cold and calculated manner of operating working places, cities, and countries.

The subject of capitalism is seen by many as a confusing

subject, as it evolved with the development of the free market and our society. The concept of capitalism before the mid-19th century and after it has changed and evolved drastically. It's important to understand that by itself, capitalism isn't a bad economic philosophy. Originally, it promoted the progress of local populations through expansion of plural local businesses for the sake of creating employment. This is positive as long as the idea of profit doesn't exist as its first purpose.

Let's start with the original concept of capitalism. During its development, the marketplace was drastically different. This kind of capitalism is part of a reality which has been irrelevant to our reality for a very long time. The original concept of capitalism is old, dating from the mid-16th century. It assumes that a social structure exists in which each person chooses the work for themselves or for someone else. It evolved during a period in which opening a business and owning a new store was not as easy as today. The assumption was that a formal education system like today's didn't exist and that the opportunity available to individuals was relative to the time and location. In such a world, a hairdresser that suddenly had more customers could do two things: keep the extra income for themselves and put it in a safe place, or invest by hiring another employee and making the business expand. Income that's not taken by the owner but is reinvested in the business is called capital. Originally, the creation of capital didn't concentrate on making the owner a profit, but instead it focused on creating capital to reinvest for the benefit of society. This concept is based on an economic idea that capital should promote employment and progress while adding value to the owner as a business person.

Without a doubt, such a philosophy promotes the concentration of power. But, as we'll see, as long as the size of the market is limited, and the population is professionalized in specific occupations, the capacity to create a concentration of power is limited. Such a limitation cannot create a danger to its population as long as each person invests in their own field. The early stages of capitalism pushed the rapid evolution of the Western world and promoted the wellbeing of its populations in the evolving new mega cities.

Since those days, capitalism has evolved and taken a new form. The creation of the Western empire, the Industrial Revolution, the creation of democracies, and the technological revolution all allowed the use of a good philosophy to lead to a bad practice. The use of capitalism for the sake of creating profit has changed the world and reshaped it into the world we live in today. As we'll see in the next chapter, the emergence of globalization as a means of exploitation is not a matter of conspiracy or secret, but a slow evolution of a well-planned mechanism.

The economic war on the market domination has brought a new way of trade that's never existed before in human history. The old concept of capitalism was an economic philosophy introduced for a limited market of a small group of business owners, while the new capitalism is a psychosocial philosophy requiring an unlimited market and imposed on every individual in the social system. In the evolution of capitalist ideas, capital has been converted into profit. The capacity of capitalism to emerge as the main way of doing business around the world requires a better understanding regarding the evolution of the monetary system. As money is the basic tool moving both the old and new capitalism, understanding how money evolved will help us better understand the new capitalistic ideology of the modern world.

The Evolution of Our Monetary System

Let's start by the definition of money. As described in the book *Sapiens* by Yuval Noah Harari, money "is not coins and banknotes. Money is anything that people are willing to use in order to represent systematically the value of other things for the purpose of exchanging goods and services. Money enables people to compare quickly and easily the value of different commodities." From that definition, we can conclude that an economic system doesn't require the existence of money, but money without an economy doesn't exist. The concept of coinage has been created for the ease of commerce between humans, as all alternatives were too complicated to handle. Many alternatives existed before the arrival of the coinage around the world, from Cowry shells to pepper to grains. Finally, after the growth of our populations from small communities to cities, the need for a fixed and trusted exchange commodity brought humanity to create trade by coins.

At the beginning of its existence, money as coins was a commodity by itself. It's called a commodity because the creation of a gold coin requires labor for mining the gold and shaping the coins themselves. As this process isn't different from any other manufacturing process, coinage is seen as a product like any other. As long as the money was represented by a material product, the understanding of the money concept by the masses was realistic and controlled like any other commodity.

In its early stages, money wasn't different from any other product in trade, as it required time for production and time to physically move it from hand to hand. Those requirements restricted the usage of money to its actual quantity and physical ownership. In that period, the trust in coins was absolute, as it was handled immediately and valued by the local kings. The exchange of physical coins has maintained a healthy trade between humans for thousands of years. During the 17th century, a shift in the European monetary system has been ignored by many as a dramatic event in human trade. The exchange of money from gold and silver coin to paper (called banknotes) that represented an amount of physical gold held by a certain bank given in paper form to its original owner. This change was the first step to the devaluation of the money itself, as the actual exchange of money between individuals became not physical, but socially agreed.

To make this point clear, we can look at the next example. There's one bank in a certain town that prints paper bills representative of the gold deposited by individuals in the town. As all the citizens believe in the security of the bank, the majority have put their gold in the bank in exchange for banknotes. At this moment, the majority of the gold isn't actually moving, and trade is done with representative paper. In this new form of trading, trade is based on a social agreement and not based on actual commodities. By itself, this version of trade isn't negative and can even make the trading easier. In this manner, there's no need for the circulation of metal anymore, which is more comfortable and safe. As long as the banknote represents actual gold in the bank, and the bank doesn't use the gold for its own benefit, the notes are accepted by everyone in the market, and the old balance of trade is still possible. This change is mainly a psychological change, not an economical one.

The second change in the monetary system happened many years after the creation of banknotes. This time, it wasn't a change related to the physical objects in trade, but to the value of the piece itself. This occurred at the beginning of the 20th century. During that period, the exchange of the value of the paper money changed to be valued not by gold in deposit, but by a certain value prescribed by the government. This first happened in the USA in 1971, led by president Nixon, and called the "The Nixon Shock." Over two years, the concept of money as bills transformed from a gold-related currency to a "floating currency." A floating currency is a type of exchange rate regime in which a currency value fluctuates in response to foreign exchange market mechanisms. This was a drastic change, and it was the first time that money didn't represent a direct outcome of actual commodities in hand, but was based on market values. Until today, the global trade of natural resources isn't made based on a comparable value of labor required, but is based on the value of the dollar.

At the first step of evolution, the change from metal

money to paper money didn't, by itself, change the conceptual idea of money for the masses, but did impose it as a representative tool. This change is important mainly regarding the immediate value of commodities, as the trade changed from a value in hand to a value they didn't possess in hand. Changing the value of money from a material commodity to a variable currency controlled by the government and banks made no real change in the eyes of the masses in the first place. This change created a new era in which governments and banks work hand-in-hand to control the value of the individual production process and the earning of individual incomes. This new economic system gave the banks an arbitrary power on the value of its citizens' income and created a direct, inseparable connection between the fate of the bank, the government, and the citizens. For the masses, the trade of a cheap commodity (represented as paper bills) that do not inherently have value is the first of two steps in the long process of the devaluation of the monetary system which brings the monetary system one step closer to being nothing but a conceptual idea accepted by the masses as a representation of things they all wish to have.

The last and most influential change exchanged paper money for virtual money, and happened only recently. By converting the monetary system into an electronic one, money lost its value as a commodity, as no manufacturing, natural resources, or laborers are required for its creation. This devaluation of the monetary system allows the amount of money in the market to grow to proportions that don't make sense to the individual nor to its requirement itself. Based on data from December 2013, the United States has $10.5 trillion in circulation with only $1.2 trillion printed. This gap between printed money and circulating money is a big part of the possibilities available to create debts paid by the individual citizens through different taxes, which impoverish their reality without having a real understanding of why or how it happened in this way. Just to be clear with the years passing the amount of actual printed money in diminishing constantly. Certain appreciation has been made regarding this subject, proposing the cash money will disappear from circulation no later than 2035.

The process of devaluation of the monetary system was extremely important for the capitalistic evolution and the acceptance of the conceptual idea of inflation. It allows and exploits excessive debt and simplifies the philosophy that an individual, as part of a country, can live based on money they don't actually have. The devaluation of the monetary system brought the money to be perceived by the individual as an abstractive concept that cannot be touched, controlled, or understood, while being the main necessity to maintain one's survival. Such a reliance on conceptual ideas has only been seen in relation to gods.

Money no longer gives value to the work of a professional. Its evolution and devaluation become the tools controlling the lives of individuals instead of supporting them. Capitalism brought individuals to believe that money is the cause of and the reason for their happiness, misery, and success. These days, a tool that was created for the benefit of society has become a tyrant. A system based on interest rates, credits, and loan is a monetary system that is constantly evolving in a clear direction, a system in which money creates itself by the existence of time, unrelated to the people using it.

The Era of Social Capitalism

The one who sees social isolation as the end of everything he values, and would rather live as a slave to a system than die a free master of his own existence, will become the engine of the slavery of a social system.

The Marketplace

"New age capitalism" can be defined as an economic and political system in which a country's trade and industry are controlled by private owners for the purpose of creating profit. To create and maintain such a system, an initial investment of capital is required in an operation (start-ups, stores, governments, projects, etc.) for the creation of a surplus (called capital). For the creation of profit, a surplus is required in a working place. The idea of a surplus can be understood as the creation of extra money above the necessary cost of production. This means the creation of extra income in the process of the creation of the product itself. To create such a cycle of excess money, there are a few options available for the capitalist. These options are:

- **Reducing the cost of the manufacturing or importation of products.** This kind of surplus can be created by reducing the price of materials required for production, or by reducing expenses related to the local commerce and importation laws.

- **Reducing the cost of the employment while keeping the product price as it was.** This method requires the reduction of labor cost without reflecting that change in the final product price.

- **Increasing the price of the product while keeping the same manufacturing costs.** This method is done by convincing a population to pay a higher price for products.

These techniques for creating surplus require an operating market in the first place. If no market exists, none of the above options are even possible. In many cases, the process of creating surplus requires a certain devaluation of the current reality. How this is done? To understand, we'll first examine how a marketplace work.

The basic assumption of a healthy marketplace is that the total amount of money in the market reflects and represents the value of the commodities (products) in the market. To simplify, calculate the total number of products and their prices to know how much money exists in a market. By giving products a fixed value based on the working time of the employees and the cost of the natural resources required for production, the amount of money in a market can be clear and stable. In such a system, as long as there's a constant circulation of money between the working people going to the market as buyers and sellers, a balance will be created. Such a balance allows everyone to have enough money for their basic needs of life in a healthy society.

Let's take the time to understand this idea better. To understand how a market works, it's important to understand the concept of submarket and their connections. An industry is built from many processes operating simultaneously and independently from each other, these processes can be called submarkets. For example, in the bread industry, many submarkets exist, like the wheat market, the milk market, the egg market, the employment market, and many more. Each of the submarkets functions with and thanks to other submarkets, which create the industry itself when combined. A submarket like the milk market can be operated as submarket of many industries. The individual milk farm is not considered a submarket, but is taking an active part in the creation of the submarket itself.

In a general, in a marketplace, multitudes of final products are offered to potential buyers. Those products are all submarkets of the bigger marketplace. In such a market, a seller in a submarket will be the buyer in another one. For example, an employee in a shoes store is part of the employment submarket by trading their time for income. Going to the market for groceries makes our shoes seller a buyer in the submarket of groceries. It's simple to understand, as an employee is selling their time to the employer, and the employee later goes to the market place later on to buy groceries with the money they made from their employment.

In a small, limited market, as long as the money constantly circulates between the submarkets, equilibrium will be maintained. An individual owning a business that employs other people to create a better product will keep the market in balance as long as the owner takes a salary equivalent to the value of their work as an employee. In such a marketplace, a person who wants more income can work more or professionalize in a specific field, as long as they're spending their income immediately for the sake of the circulation, a balance will be kept. As the market is a living organism evolving based on its movement, the basic rule of a healthy economy demands a constant movement of money. From the moment one person in the market decide they want some savings, a blockage of money will be created due to lack of circulation in the market. Such a blockage of funds brings an immediate reaction observed as a shortage of money for the rest of the market itself.

Let's look at a simple example with a market of 10 people and 30 gold coins are valued at 1. The requirements for a good standard of living for each individual is three coins each. Each person is manufacturing a different product and selling it to the extra nine people in the market. As long as the people are constantly exchanging the coin between themselves, they always each have three coins, which will be reflected in products or coins. From the moment one of the person decides that he would like to own five coins and starts to accumulate it, there will be a shortage of two coins in the market circulation.

In a marketplace in which resources are limited, the concentration of resources by one person or group will immediately create a shortage for the others. This point is easy to understand, but missed somehow when looking at our lives today. The size of the market isn't relevant to this principal. As long as the resources are limited, the rule will apply.

For the sake of keeping it simple, we will keep those market principles in mind. Any market can be seen as the main market of some submarket or be seeing as a submarket of a bigger one. The principle of a balanced market will always be valid regardless of its size.

The Creation of Profit

Creating profit that doesn't already exist requires a change in the market. Smaller markets have the advantage of operating as a community, which protects them from individual fraud. The bigger the market, the harder it will be for individuals to affect the changes needed for the creation of profit. Let's see how it works. When the idea of profit arises in a market, two options exist to achieve such this goal. The first is to reduce the cost required for the creation of the product. In this case, the cost of the manufacturing will diminish, while the market price stays the same. The second option is to increase the price of the commodities without having to increase the manufacturing cost.

The idea of profit is based on a fundamental idea called employment or market isolation. If an individual works for themselves manufacturing chairs, this individual will use only the time required to manufacture, the cost of their working hours, and the cost of the natural resources required for the job. No profit will be created by the individual work. On the other hand, thanks to their income, they'll still be able to live well. A fisherman who fishes by himself and makes a good living can make some good money not considered a profit.

By calculating the price of the fishes sold relatively for the cost of the fuel, boat, and nets, we can calculate the fisherman's wage per hour. It's an important point to understand before we continue. Some occupations are valued more than others. This is reflected in their income per hour. The ability to generate a good income per hour doesn't make it profit. It's very simple: the cost of products needs to reflect the cost of natural resources required to build the product, compensate the time worked, and the effort put in the process. A certain professionalization in this case is considered as a natural resource. An expert heart surgeon doesn't make profit by performing surgery. Rather, he is generating an income. The cost of the operation should be valued by the cost of the material and space required combined with his unique capacities enquired by time and effort spend previously to the operation.

Let's look at the chair maker again. Under the assumption that he works in a place he owns, the cost of the chairs for the chair maker will stem from the material needed for the manufacturing process. This will include the wood bought, nails, and the machinery costs. From there, this calculation is quite simple. Following this calculation, we can add the time worked to the manufacturing cost. The final sale price, in general, will be fixed by the market and the buyer. The chair maker, for his part, will try to sell it as expensive as possible to reflect the cost of his working hours. If we assume that no transportation costs are required for bringing the chairs to the market, the final selling price minus the manufacturing cost will determine the hourly income of the chair maker. If the product quality is high, the chair maker can earn more per hour, which still won't make it a profit. This distinction is important, as it differs between a hardworking man who earns well for his job and a capitalist making profit on his investment.

From this rule, for the creation of profit, there must be a creation of a gap between the manufacturing cost and the product cost at market. How is this done? It all comes to the devaluation of employment and the separation of people and their natural resources.

Understanding the concept of employment is crucial. Employment is a relationship between two parties, usually based on a contract where work is paid for. One party, which may be a corporation, for-profit, not-for-profit organization, co-operative or other entity, is the employer and the other party is the employee.

Employees work in return for payment, which may be in the form of an hourly wage, by piecework, or an annual salary, depending on the type of work an employee does or which sector they work in. In some fields, employees may receive gratuities, bonus payment, or stock options. In some types of employment, employees receive benefits in addition to payment. To make it simple, employment is an agreement made between an individual and their employer, in which a certain amount of payment is agreed in exchange for the time and capacity of the employee. This process, in many cases, has the employee play a specific role in the creation of products, owned by the employer.

For the purpose of creating profit, the price of employment must be unrelated to the number of products or cost created, as they're paid hourly. Eventually, the creation of profit is the creation of extra income for sales above the total cost of employment and manufacturing. The important conclusion we need to keep is that, for the sake of the creation of income for the employer, the employee will be obliged to work extra manufacturing hours to create this income (called surplus) for the employer.

The creation of income without being an active part of manufacturing is possible, but only by diminishing the income of another person in the manufacturing process or reducing manufacturing costs. I'm referring to manufacturing here as it's simple to understand. In real life, miners, transportation people, sales people, builders, and so on are all employees that can be manipulated for the sake of employer profit. Profit creation opportunities are very limited in a communal market. Buyers can compare the price and quality of similar products in the market, and can compare employment wage, which limits the possibility to create profit. So, how does it work and how can capitalism manage to create profit?

Let's take back the two options of profit unrelated to the

employment cost above and try to apply them into our market. By making product prices higher, the immediate outcome is predicated as a massive drop in sales. Let's use bananas as an example. In markets in which several people are selling the same bananas, an increase in the price of a commodity doesn't make sense in the eyes of the buyer that can go and buy the same commodity next door at a lower price. We can apply this to any product, even iPhones. If three stores are selling the same iPhone, and one store sells it at a higher price, people will buy from the business with the lowest price.

The second option available for profit creation is lowering the cost of natural resources. Let's go back to our bananas. The options are to bring lower quality bananas and keep the high price, or to try to find a cheaper way to bring the bananas to the store, which will normally take more time and bring older bananas. Under the same assumption made above, if the quality of a product drops but the price stays high, following a short period of trial and self-realization, the consumers will go to the neighboring store and buy from there.

The last option available is to lower the cost of employment needed for manufacturing. A devaluation of the employment price is indeed very effective and probably the best option to create profit. Capitalists have two tools available for this devaluation: blurring the individual's understanding of the worth of their time, or blurring their ability to evaluate manufacturing costs. The success of these tools will be reflected in lowering the employee's hourly wage, which will inevitably force the employee to work more hours for the same price. To make it simple, if a shop owner who sells bananas manages to pay employees less, they can keep good quality bananas at competitive prices, which generates profit and is still accepted by market consumers.

To create such a change in the market, a very important process must happen: the separation of the employee from their natural resources and their understanding of their worth. Without the ability of an individual to work by themselves with the natural resources around them, that individual will be forced to enter the employment cycle for income. In such a market, the employee's capacity to bargain wages will be un-proportional to the employer's power. The creation of a society in which the individual is obliged to sell their time for the sake of maintaining their lifestyle will be created. As the individual lacks the capacity to maintain a lifestyle without the obligation of selling their time, a perfect system will be created for the exploitation of the employee and the creation of profit.

In a society ruled by the capitalist scheme, an educational system will be created to teach the young generation that their best option for success is to enter the employment cycle. In such a society, no effort will be required for the creation of profit, as the separation of the people and their natural resources and the willingness of the young to enter the employment cycle will be a matter of the reality of the community. A practical example is the next one. In the USA, a college and university education are required to get a good job with a sufficient income. At the same time, to get a good education, a lot of money is required. In many cases, a loan will be required for the studies. At the end of those studies, the young educated person will be obliged to enter the employment cycle first to pay back his debts and secondly to maintain himself. This is just one simple example for the vicious capitalistic system.

The Outcome of Establishing the Profit Structure in a Balanced Market

Profit creation is impossible in a balanced and free market without creating a chain of events that affects the entire market. As we concluded above, in a balanced market, there's no space for profit.

Profit creation will immediately create a shortage in the system. In the market, all submarkets are related, as they support each other. The crash of a submarket will inevitably create a shortage in the rest of the submarkets. As a rule, creating a profit in a balanced market will diminish the pluralism of businesses and create a concentration of power by the profit maker.

Let's understand why. When there's a profit in a balanced market, it creates an income shortage in one of its submarkets. This shortage will prevent from the seller in a submarket from having the income needed to buy from another submarket. A lack of buyers in submarkets will push the seller to find alternative income sources. This cycle of impoverishment can work as well in a market that already has employees. Let's take an example from our life. If the salary of a bartender drops, they won't be able to buy their normal groceries in the supermarket, which will create an income loss in the supermarket section as well.

In case the seller has his own employees and the sales are dropping, he'll have two options available: lower the quality of his product or the wage of his employees. In many cases, the owner of the supermarket will have to employ fewer people, which will affect their income and they won't spend as much money at the bar, which then creates another shortage for the bartender, who then buys less in the supermarket. This cycle can be called "the cycle of impoverishment."

Indeed, we see a disconcerting pattern in such a cycle. In case the seller isn't employing people, he'll have no choice but to become an employee for someone else as he can't maintain his own business.

From the moment the mechanism of profit starts, the evolution of the market becomes quite clear. In this cycle, the employment of others gives small business owners the chance to lower his employees' salaries before closing his store and joining the employment pool. As we saw, the entire market and its submarkets are connected. The creation of the rat race after profit in one submarket will inevitably bring a change to all the market. This kicks off a long process of employee impoverishment, closure of small businesses, and decreased product variety and quality. Such a process can be called "the impoverishment cycle of the capitalism." During this process. two groups will be created: the employees and the employers. Such a separation is necessary for the creation and maintenance of profit, as the market is changing and feeding the capitalist scheme.

To efficiently maintain the capitalist scheme of profit creation, only two kinds of people can exist. The division is clear: the ones making profit on the time of others, and the ones selling their time. Grouping employees and employer makes everything much easier. The employee working in a "profit based economy" will work for the profit of his employer, while receiving an income that he'll spend at another business for the sake of the profit of the employer of the other shop. Operating a society this way for a long period of time will create a natural cycle in which the employer will inevitably accumulate more profit, while the employees will work more, earn less, and will be at the hands and mercy of the employer as a way of life.

Now we can better understand the chain of the pursuit of profit:

- In a limited market, the creation of profit by one organization or individual will create a shortage in the market. More profit will be made, and there will be fewer funds available for the rest of the market.
- This shortage will create falling sales in the submarkets.
- The submarket will not be able to support employment and will start affecting the employees in the stores.

- Less money will be in circulation, and small shop owners will have less income. This lack of income will force small businesses to close and join the employment pool.
- A cycle of impoverishment and shortage will arise, known as an "economic crisis," creating a clear separation between employer and employees.
- A clear separation between the employer and employee's classes will be created and sustained by its own existence.

In the 21st century, the devaluation of the monetary system and the enlargement of local market to global one, have created the perfect foundation for the creation of the capitalist scheme.

The Need of Capitalism for Globalization

As we saw in previous sections, the capitalist scheme in a small and closed market is very limited. Capitalism as a form of business is limited as long as the resources of the manufacturer are limited, the money in the society is limited, and society is aware of the disastrous effect of exploitation. During periods in which markets were small and the commerce options were limited, there was a general reluctance by the population regarding the idea of profit. Conversation about the dangers of the pursuit of profit has existed for many years and can even be found in Aristotle's writings.

As long as manufacturing capacity is heavily based on human capacity and the market size is limited, the profit creation remains limited and steady. Imperialism and the industrial revolution have allowed for the creation of new capitalist advantages. Those came in the form of inquiring machines that would replace the need for a professional human labor and the arrival of slaves. The global trade that has evolved in the last 300 years and the invention of machinery broke the chain of limited markets and created a new kind of market for the pursuit of profit.

The capitalistic manufacturing has grown hand-in-hand with the growth of the European empires. That evolution solidified capitalism as the main economic philosophy in the Western market. The study of this period is both fascinating and terrifying, as we can see step-by-step how the capitalist scheme created legislation supporting the profit creation.

An important point has to be made: a limited market can create a limited profit. A communal market exists to protect all players, as the pursuit of profit is antisocial and contradictory to the common good. For the survival and evolution of capitalism, the market must continue to grow. This enlargement of markets has taken shape as "globalization."

The Consequences of a Capitalistic Global Market

Human empires have always tried to take over and rule the world's populations. In many cases, the ruling empire believed that it had conquered all the known world. The idea of bringing all humans under one ruler or entity can be called "globalization." This concept is as old as humanity and it's what the empires have kept in mind during many conquests. Looking at it from that perspective, it's safe to say that the concept of globalization and its evolution is a natural process pursued by humanity during its evolution. The fascinating thing about the empires of ancient times is that from a certain point, the reasons to continue the imperial conquest had little to do with the need to get richer, but rather the will to unify all of humanity under one entity.

For individuals born in the capitalistic era, the idea that the conquest of ancient empires was unrelated to profit can be surprising and hard to grasp. There's no doubt that at the first conquest, the riches won indeed played a big role, but if the purpose of the conquerors was only profit, the cost of expansion and risks involved in war wouldn't be worth the actual riches obtained from a certain point. Looking back on history, we see that the majority of empires were mainly after the unification of the world as they knew it. Those empires always believed that the unification of all its subjects would be possible if the populous adopted the philosophy of the empire. Not all historians agree on this perspective, but there's evidence of this in all empires unrelated to their location and time.

The course of the general unification of humans has progressed slowly over thousands of years. Every empire that has risen and fallen has left some common concepts and culture that integrated into the local societies throughout its conquered land. The empire of modern times exists thanks to the capitalist scheme. Thanks to the rise of the Western world and its technology, we're now closer than ever to globalization. The tools that bring us towards global unification are not always the one we should keep once our goals are achieved. After all, we wouldn't keep a raft that helps us cross a river if we know no more rivers will come. It is a very simple logic. We all agree that some challenges require specific tool for solving the problems. Those tools are important as they allow us to overcome certain situations. From the other side, keeping the tool when the problem no longer exists makes the journey more complicated and sometimes, impossible.

The idea that a tool that was practical for a specific problem becomes the problem after it's used for many generations is not surprising. Many books have been written about this idea in the Buddhist and eastern cultures.

Global unification was pursued in the past based on the willingness of an elite group to control and enrich itself. Those ideas don't benefit any people outside of that minority, as it's not done based on principals like the wellbeing of the globe or its inhabitants, but is based on the greed of individuals at the cost of hurting people and the planet.

The conversations and information spread around in recent years about global warming are just a part of the problems created by the current control of the Western empire. The illogical arguments regarding the validity of the information verifying global warming is ridiculous. The argument between politicians regarding the existence of global warming are nothing but a brutal way to hide the facts behind the ruin of the globe for profit. Even if we decide to ignore the subject of global warming, many other problems have been created following the pursuit of profit, which can be proven and showed easily. The pollution in cities, the pollution of water and nature by our factories, and the extinction of various species around us are just some of the consequences of blind pursuit of global profit.

The globalization of commerce in recent years allows a new network of trade that can benefit the world. During the history of humans, the limitations in trade, language, and geographic location created a limitation of resources for local populations. Those limitations could bring a leader to decide to go to war to increase resources. The lack of logistical structure to move merchandise limited the capacity of goods and products to reach far destinations. Thanks to the capitalist evolution led by the Western empire, the ability to produce products, ship them safely and efficiently, and preserve the products in the process created a new era in which the idea of limited resources in a specific market has become a matter of decision and not a matter of incapability. It's true that the cost of these resources, in many cases, is not affordable for a local market. But as we will see, the problem is not the process or the availability, but a lack of willingness of the elite to reduce its profit for the benefit of the rest of the people. The global network achieved in the 21st century is efficient, healthy, and productive for the entire population. The way we use our new network is the main complication we currently face.

As we mentioned previously, the pursuit of profit in a limited market has clear boundaries. If the pursuit of profit is made aggressively in a limited market, the system of enrichment will create a progressive concentration of power which will eventually collapse the market. The new globalization trading channels have removed all boundaries from the limitation of natural resources existing in local markets. The ability to import and export resources and products is just one aspect of the benefits created by globalization. As a first step, the capacity to export allows manufacturers to produce in larger quantities. And, importation allows manufacturers to buy natural resources from cheaper suppliers. In the market of natural resources, very similar to the marketplace next to your house, buying bigger quantities normally reduces the cost of a single unit. The capacity for a local manufacturer to import cheaper machines and natural resources allows manufacturers to produce larger quantities and sell to more customers globally. This is the first step for maintaining and enlarging the capitalist scheme of pure profit.

Thanks to the success of the capitalist scheme in the new global market, there's a concentration of power rooted in the world's mentality. The process of importation evolved for a few decades, changing the rules of the old market, and creating a new form. The capacity to import and export has brought many benefits to the Western world. A large quantity of new products being sold in local markets was the first step of the globalized market. As more products arrived and a variety of new stores have been created, which created more jobs and more consumption volume. In the second step, the capacity of companies to manufacture enormous quantities with cheap employment from the other side of the world has reduced the price of manufacturing to an uncompetitive price for local manufacturers. Having the ability to sell the same product cheaper in a market is one of the ways to create profit. By itself, it shouldn't be seen as a negative change, as it allows the local population to save money. It's true to say that as long as the cheaper product is imported by local business, and the import is equally possible to all business owners, the ability to sell the same quality of product at a cheaper price benefits the entire population.

From the other side, in case the manufacture enters new markets by themselves, the local store won't have the ability to compete. Such an entry of an international player into the local market will inevitably bring to the closure of the majority of the small and medium business as they will progressively lose their previous advantage. In recent years, the entry of international brands into local markets created an immediate chain reaction that resulted in the closure of local small and medium businesses. This went hand-in-hand with a fall in the price of the commodities below a reasonably competitive price and the appearance of low quality products. This effect is valid in all the markets and submarkets. Example for it are brands like H&M, Primemark, all foreign supermarket brands, department stores like mediamarekt, and fast food like McDonald's, KFC and many more. As we've seen earlier in this chapter, this process of impoverishment of the local community and reduction of the number of stores are exactly the changes needed for the control of the capitalist structure of profit on the market.

It's important to understand that from the moment global expansion is available to big corporation, the mathematical scheme of capitalism doesn't require a person or country to survive and is easily spread and implement in any country as long as the local government is weak or fragile. Allowing the importation of cheap natural resources or the relocation of the manufacturing line itself to other countries inevitably creates direct unemployment across the local market related to that specific industry. Many submarkets are creating a main market, and the closure of one local submarket will inevitably bring the closure of other related submarkets. From the moment natural resources that exist in the market are imported, the income of the local, independent industry will lose income. This is easy to trace in industries like agriculture and clothing. The relocation of part or all of the manufacturing line to another market directly causes unemployment to rise. A high level of unemployment creates the foundation for big corporations to enter local markets. The entry of multinational corporations to any market brings cheap, varied products manufactured elsewhere. This directly affects the income of local merchants, who eventually close their businesses due to reduced income. The closure of those small and medium businesses is one of the biggest reasons for a drastic shift in unemployment numbers, as the shop owner and their employees are entering the cycle of unemployment. Unemployment and the arrival of multinational corporations decreases employee wages, as mainly unprofessional manpower is needed and profit must be maintained. It is important to mention that the newly unemployed population that arose from this process is normally the middle-class population, which is the core of the power of the democracy in their local governments. This phenomenon can be observed in cities around the world.

The closure of small businesses following the market entry of corporations creates a very important socio-political effect. The heart of a democratic nation is with its middle class. As the rich have the power and means to enslave the poor, there must be a strong middle class to sustain the democratic foundation of the nation. Democracy is based on the decision of the majority, for the benefit of its population as a whole. Without a strong middle class to maintain democracy, the foundation of the institution trembles and gives the self-interested elite more power. The closure of small businesses and private stores not only breaks the equilibrium of a local market, but simultaneously promotes the destruction of the middle class and the healthy political democratic foundation of the government.

Imports and Exports: Good Tools in the Wrong Hands

(This section is heavier and can be skipped if world trade is completely foreign to you and makes you sweat)

The general idea of globalization is positive if used outside of the capitalist scheme, there's a fundamental point about imports and exports to understand, which is one of the foundation for healthy globalization. For the sake of maintaining a free global trade of resources, we must understand the geographic division of humanity to optimize the system. Such a system is necessary for the sake of preventing waste or profit for the wrong organization. A trade of limited goods distributed based on a constant movement of the consumer will inevitably create unnecessary gaps between the producer and the consumer, which concentrate the producer's power and generate waste. As any kind of movement requires resources, a system in which the products and the consumer are constantly moving will undoubtedly generate waste. As humans are the only species generating waste that's not consumed by different entities later on, it can be easily agreed that the fundamental idea of the creation of waste is unnatural and negative to both humans and nature.

Moreover, it's important to mention that in case a country doesn't possess natural resources, or the number of employees needed for local manufacturing, the import of resources is the best option for the general population. Such importation is based on the needs of the local population and doesn't take into consideration the economic needs of other countries that cannot compete with a low price of the capitalist scheme. The exportation of products is healthy as long as it's used as a tool in a market that doesn't have the capacity to manufacture the commodities or doesn't have the natural resources needed. To promise a balanced market, which includes international trading, the cost of importing should always be in balance with the income from exporting of a country.

Overproduction for the purpose of reducing product costs isn't a good reason to export, as it's only being done to create profit for a few people. To maintain positive commerce in an import/export system, the overproduction must be made following a request from another market that cannot create the commodity from the first place, and never the opposite. Let's take the time to understand why should a market might require imports. One reason is based on technological development in another market. Those technological developments should improve standard of living and well-being on society. In such a case, the capacity of a company or country to create a better product will benefit the entire population. The second reason relates to the lack of natural resources of a local market. For example, let's look at the import of fruits, vegetables, petrol, etc., to markets that lack the necessary climate or resources themselves. In this case, imports should be done based on a standard of quality that promises relatively good products to the population. In both cases, importation should be done as little as possible and should concentrate on the quality of the commodity, not its cheap price. It's important to understand that manufacturing is an extremely well-calculated field. Overproduction as a reason to export is a reality that doesn't happen by mistake, and is enacted by self-interested capitalists in pursuit of profit.

One of the common explanations given today in support of the capitalist system is that in a competitive world, exportations from one country strengthens the local economy. They explain that thanks to exports and imports, the government has the capacity to lower taxes. Unfortunately, such an argument is based on a self-concentrated, isolated way of looking at a world economic system. As we saw previously, in a market place, the concentration of riches on one side of the world will inevitably create the impoverishment in another place.

A local market that becomes part of a global market under the capitalistic trade gives the capitalist all the tools needed to dramatically increase their profit while killing the local market. The import of products provides capitalists with the following opportunities:

1. Cheaper natural resources in other countries, even if produced in the local market.
2. Cheaper labor at the cost of unemployment in the local market.
3. The creation of multinational organizations that allow the capitalists to be unaffected by local market failures and avoid local taxation.

The development of such a process and its consequences is slow but certain. The longer the market is part of the capitalistic optimization system of profit, the more unstable the local market becomes, and the more the local market suffers from dependence on the global market. This process can be seen not only in the Western world, but can be seen in all countries that are part of the capitalist global market. Tom Burgis wrote an enlightening book called *The Looting Machine*, which describes the disastrous consequences of the process of the capitalist system in Africa and how it's been created from the moment of independence in each country with the assistance and support of the Western world. The misperception of the situations in Africa and Asia, and the reason for this situation in the Western world, is one of the clearest signs of the elite controlling and understanding of the population regarding the new global system.

The spiral evolution of the capitalist global trap is simple and easy to measure in any economy and market:

- Balanced local market maintains a healthy market based on its natural resources and man power
- Opening of the import/export trade to the global multinational corporations occurs under the guise of progress and optimization

- Entrance of multinational corporations to the market and the creation of bureaucratic automatic jobs for low wages and short contracts
- Devaluation of local production following the lowest available prices from other markets
- Incapability of small businesses to compete with the corporate prices, leading to their closures
- Death of local industries that cannot compete with low import prices
- Creation of massive unemployment, which boosts the income of the corporations as the only cheap commodities available are corporate products
- Increase of unemployment and collapse of the middle class
- Market optimization in which the majority of the market is employed in a specific domain controlled by capitalistic corporations
- Creation of a global net profit that is stronger than the local government and unaffected by local market economic fluctuations

By allowing such an evolution, developments will inevitably make the market to be dependent on the global market and the local riches. This reality will create an unstable local economy that no longer has the capacity to disconnect itself from the global market. This cycle is a wonderful example of how a minority of individuals can create good tools and use them badly. Looking at the world today, it's easy to see how the global market mainly benefits the corporations and their beneficiaries, but don't benefit the new global cities and their citizens.

The conclusion we're trying to get to is not that imports and exports should be avoided. As a matter of fact, it is part of the natural evolution of humans and essential for positive globalization. The point is that it's a matter of how and why a country is importing and exporting goods and resources. It is important to understand that importing and exporting is positive as long as a country's exports are equal to the imports. If a country exports more than it imports, it means another country must do the opposite. Balance is very important in all sizes of markets. An imbalance in the import/export scale will always promise imbalance in another place. As long as a governmental system exists to promise the equal amount of imports and exports, trade can be maintained as positive for the population in the long run both locally and globally.

Capitalism and Government

Throughout history, humans have managed themselves socially through monarchies. Whether the rulers were called king, emperor, or lord, the reigns of a single leader have demanded rulers to accumulate money, land, and power. It's not clear if the process of achieving the throne made kings rich, or if it is the riches that allowed the ruler to gain this position, as he could hire mercenaries and buy land. Probably, in some cases it was the first, and in some cases, the other. Those rulers have one thing in common. Monarchs were required to seize power and money for the sake of increasing their ability to maintain their power. For centuries, the position of the ruler in a society gave them access to resources by means of taxes from their subjects, profit from conquests, and natural resources from the land in the kingdom. Make no mistakes, any solo ruler falls into this category, even if the ruler was considered good and kind to his subjects.

The idea of an elected house of commons or parliament is old and can be traced back to the ancient Greeks, the Roman Empire, and in England in the 13th century. Nevertheless, the social ruling structure at this period was very different from the democracy we know in modern times. Those structures used in democratic ideas in a very limited way. In most cases, the democratic rights and the opportunity to be elected has been given to a very small group of the population. Such a democratic structure was limited by a ruler's capacity to veto many laws and was almost always bound to a certain monarchy controlling the state of affairs, holding the ultimate power on the execution of the democratic decisions. It's not surprising that for the sake of controlling large populations, a population must be engaged. The creation of an institution made of the people themselves helped maintain the local leadership, and many times served as a mediator between the monarchy and its subjects. In all those democracies, the group that was allowed to participate was small, made only from men, usually white, with a higher economic status than the rest of the population. In other words, the democracies of the old days weren't close to being a form of social management in which the entire population had an equal opportunity to participate in and influence the system. Moreover, in almost all the cases, the parliament didn't hold any power to change or to force the ruling monarchy.

The democracies known to us today are new relative to our species' existence. The creation of a population led by a democratic structure without any superior monarch began at the end of the 18th century with the independence of the United States. That was less than 300 years ago, which isn't a long time compared to human evolution. Following the creation of the USA, the rest of the Western countries followed, overthrowing monarchs or making them irrelevant, and establishing a new kind of democracy in which the power over the state is held by the people themselves. In the early period of the new democracies, a bigger part of the population could take part in the democratic process than the old democracies. Nevertheless, at that stage, women, slaves, and low-income citizens still didn't hold any rights. The creation of the new democratic countries started based on principals known from ancient times, which was the only option available at that point. When studying the evolution of democracy, we can see that every time one of the democratic states changes or upgrades its system, the majority of its democratic neighbors adopted the changes almost immediately.

Since the creation of democracies, the capacity of a certain state to maintain its democratic structure for more than 50 years has been small to nonexistent. Regardless of the beliefs many people hold these days, the concept of democracy as we know it is extremely new and revolutionary. The democratic states known to us in Europe have existed for less than 100 years in Western Europe and less than 50 years in Eastern Europe. Indeed, American independence brought new ideas to the European nations, which then started doubting the need for their monarchs. The movement of Europeans towards democracy was slow and long from American independence until the fall of local monarchies. In this process, the liberation from monarchies has been followed by leadership of local dictators and single rulers, which took advantage of the space created and the incapability of the populous to be free and equal. To make this point more practical we can look at a few European countries and their last single ruler:

- Napoleon III ruled over France until the end of 1870.
- Wilhelm I ruled over Germany until the end of 1888, Wilhelm II ruled until 1918, and then Adolf Hitler ruled over until 1945.
- Benito Mussolini ruled over Italy until 1943.
- Joseph Stalin was the leader of the USSR until 1953.
- Francisco Franco ruled over Spain until 1975.
- The Ottoman Empire controlled the majority of eastern Europe until 1918.
- Quite a few east European countries were liberated only in 1992.

Considering our governing method to be evolutionary and

linear can explain the need for such a process. After all, those new democracies were philosophically opposed to monarchy in many aspects. This perspective of the evolution of our governing system is important to understand, as it holds the keys for our progress.

The creation of a democratic government is revolutionary not only because it allows the populous to choose their leaders and change them as needed, but because the fundamental idea and purpose of the ruling party is completely different. The main philosophy held by emperors and monarchies was to maintain power and enrich the elite for the sake of supporting in their ruling. In a democratic system, the actions of a government are guided by principals based on the wellbeing, prosperity, and enrichment of its population as a whole. The process of changing the governing system in such a drastic manner required an evolutionary process of trial and error. The study of the history of politics in Europe in the last 200 years shows us many parallel trials in different countries on the continent. The replacement of the monarchy by a nationalist ruler, the liberation from the ideals of nationalism, followed by the fall of the ruler and the replacement of nationalism by democratic values of freedom and equality are all different variations of the same process.

***

The entrance of the government to the cycle of the national debts allows the rich elite to take over markets under the justification of globalization. The creation of a democratic government in a global market that is occupied by the prosperity and wellbeing of its subject is still in the middle of its natural evolutionary process. As such, it's important to constantly monitor this process by clear standards and achievements. The lack of such standards allows self-interested individuals to take control and bring the population under the control of the few. The Western world has arrived at a stage of evolution in which the old system of concentrated power doesn't fit the new social system we are working so hard to achieve. Without a doubt, thousands of years of monarchy has rooted some fundamental parasite in the societies that needs to be found and eliminated.

The fusion of government and economy are one of those parasites that we're holding onto from the previous ruling systems. Based on the definition of government made in this book, which says that the government is a managing organization, can start to understand the logical process behind it. The fundamental function of a government is to create, administer, and manage all the fields related to the common wellbeing of its subjects. Governments can enact and raise taxes to acquire funds necessary to operate. Each sum that enters the government account should be invested in a clear manner, for the sake of avoiding gaps. To say it in simple words, government is, or should be, a nonprofit organization. As such, it should not occupy itself with creating surplus in its work or its citizens, as every sum taken by the government for the sake of surplus has a direct impact on the value of the income missing for the population. Moreover, the relationship between government and business are a "one direction relationship." The role of the government is to monitor the activities of businesses and make sure there's no exploitation or concentration of power. It's true to say that government intervention in the market is based on its local philosophy, which varies from country to country. But, we can all agree that the government's job should not be, in any case, involved in doing business or creating profit for itself. How did we arrive here? How did nobody notice? Those are very good questions indeed.

The creation of profit by a minority at the price of the impoverishment of others is anti-social. It's the responsibility of the government to block and fight this process. As long as the price of the natural resources and the employment rate are controlled and dictated by the local market itself, profit creation is limited. A strong government concentrated on the good of its subjects will consciously or unconsciously prevent the capitalist mechanism from exploiting natural resources or devaluing wages. By creating legislation regarding the working hours and wage of employment in the market, while maintaining a strong policy on imports/exports for the sake of the majority of the individuals, will create a natural balance that will preserve itself as a social one. It's possible that the fast evolution of capitalist globalization evolved too fast compared to the local governments' ability to understand or fight it. Or possibly, in some cases, the local government didn't understand the risk they took by accepting the new commerce philosophy. The fact is, the capitalist global scheme holds power over government, as the national debt and the self-interested rulers are suffocating the population and its future.

The national debt and the interest rates attached to it forced governments to bow to the capitalist scheme and adopt it as its main guideline of action. The existence of such national debts requires a non-profit organization to produce a surplus for the sake of its survival. Today, a country considered to have a healthy economic status is a country that manages to pay back its interest rate on the national loan. This implies a very simple point: government does not have the ability to pay back its debts. It's a loop known to many individuals, in which the need to create income doesn't improve the situation, but doesn't make it worse, either. Ignoring the questions regarding how we arrived at this point, it's quite easy to understand why governments don't manage to take themselves out of those debts. The job of a government is complicated enough without needing to maintain a profitable business, and it's absurd to believe that it will manage to do both.

The need of government to create surplus is destructive and abusive, and a process that should be avoided. In case the capitalist scheme merges with the government philosophy, the only tool a government has to create a surplus is tax collection. In today's economy, a big part of taxes taken from citizens are used to cover an interest rate of government debts. The taxes taken as high sales taxes and income taxes are a government tool that promotes unbalance and inequality in the market, as the income of the seller diminishes hand-in-hand with the increase of consumer spending. The usage of high income tax and sales tax by the government promises insufficient funds for the individual in their daily life. That is, without any doubt, increasing and accelerating the process of poverty of the population. As governments around the world are fighting to collect enough funds to pay the interest rate on their debts, they'll never come close to covering the national debts in the first place. This struggle cannot bring any positive evolution to its citizens, as it promises an increase in the taxes which just creates more poverty. This situation is known and understood by professionals and governments. Nevertheless, no actions have been taken by the majority of the countries around the globe. Solutions exist. They're not easy ones, but they exist. I truly believe that understanding the role of a government, comprehending capitalist ideas, and knowing the danger of merging the two are the first steps toward finding better solutions.

Capitalist Globalization: The New World Order

The optimization of the global market works with a known end: the creation of an unprofessional employment market with limited access to knowledge and natural resources. In the last few decades, individuals have lost their understanding of professionalism and only know the basic functions necessary to operate machinery for a given task. In a society in which the main function of humans is to operate a machine or supervise a network, without the need to understand how or why it works, the unprofessional population will certainly cooperate in exchange for employment. Such a weak population will eventually work for the price of any wage as long as it exists.

The Western world has lost its capacity to maintain itself, as it has lost its industrial power and never had its own natural resources. For the sake of its survival, the constant import of cheap commodities for the illusion of comfort of the masses continues at the cost of enslavement of Asian and African populations. Western society, by itself, doesn't manufacture the majority of what they consume, which makes them dependent on African and Asian countries. The majority of the work available in the Western world is bureaucratic, unproductive, and unnecessary to the actual survival and maintenance of a peaceful society, as the majority of commodities purchased by Westerners are commodities that don't come from any administrative work. To make this point stronger, the majority of the employment in the West is bureaucratic, while the need for an actual production force is required for the products the population consumes in a market in which the majority of individuals are incapable of creating products themselves. In such a society, the ones who control jobs and resources will control society.

Looking Forward

The conclusion taken from these ideas should not, in any case, be that the idea that imports and exports are unhealthy. As mentioned above, importing and exporting as needed can benefit the population. As seen all over this chapter, a general motive is repeating itself when approaching any field in our society. The tools acquired in the last decade have drastically increased our comfort, health, longevity, and understanding of ourselves and the world around us. The new tools of communication and connection are remarkable and can be used to benefit the entire human population. Many times, the negative use of a tool was necessary for its discovery and its positive aspect. Sometimes, it just happened to evolve attached to negative aspects.

It's important to say that as most of the progress in the last 200 years has been made thanks to research and our ability to use the new tools on large scales. Human evolution in the last two centuries has been possible only thanks to people and entities that willingly invested their capital in research and in bold navigation across the globe. There are many misconceptions about the origin of the funds invested in early research and global expeditions. Back in the early 17th century, no king or government had invested in research or long expeditions, as they were risky and costly. The majority of the funding came from investors looking for a way to increase their capital and their power. It's true to say that this investment eventually created an elite class of businesspeople and merchants that overpowered kings and kingdoms. But, due to the healthy development of the societies around that power, it was a positive process at that period.

As mentioned above, any concentration of power, especially economic, is unsocial and dangerous. From the other side, as long as the purpose of the investment is done for the sake of more investment, no profit is made. If there's no profit being made, there should be no concentration of money. There's nothing wrong with letting the people who know how to lead do their job. But, it is a problem to allow to any individual or entity to accumulate wealth. Capitalism brought us to our modern world, and should be appreciated for its contributions to humanity. From the other side, the idea of profit, or the use of capitalism to create profit and enrich a select few, is dangerous and should be prevented.

The fact that we became a global community doesn't mean that our resources are unlimited. In fact, at any given moment, resources are always limited in some way. The belief that we'll manage to find more or dig up more resources is theoretical at best and doesn't promise material results. As any market is always limited, it has the same rules of any limited system when it comes to balancing the system. We know that at any given time, enough resources already exist for the entire population on Earth to live well. The only possible explanation for the lack of resources in the majority of the world is the creation of unbalance and concentration of resources by the few. In fact, based on a New York Times report dating July 2017, there are 2,000 billionaires in the world. The value of the 10 richest persons in the world together is $670 billion US dollars. It's difficult to understand how much money that actually is. Based on publications made by www.visionofearth.org, a calculation has been made that shows that to end extreme poverty worldwide in 20 years, the total cost per year would be about $175 billion. This represents less than one percent of the combined income of the richest countries in the world. Moreover, the total funds required during those 20 years don't surpass the total sum of profit held by those 2,000 billionaires mentioned above. This is just a fast illustration of the rule of equilibrium existing in current global market.

Before going to the streets and asking for those 2,000 people's wallets, it's important to understand what we are angry about. A system made for the sake of prosperity requires a socially aware movement. As our population grows, so does the market. The need for new jobs and progress is part of our daily life, as we are constantly growing and consuming more. A system that creates surplus in a fair way—meaning that the surplus itself doesn't come from the impoverishment of the employees or the decrease in the quality of our products—can be positive and even required. The only limitation to such capital is that it must be reinvested into the system to create more decent jobs and benefit the population itself. As any other system, capitalism as a philosophy for a global economy is not bad. The main problem with the system itself is the creation of profit for limited groups and individuals.

The economic world we live in is more in our imagination than in the world around us. In reality—as any other imaginary aspect—it can have practical effect only if we accept it and maintain the idea. Companies and corporations are entities that don't really exist and don't pay for their mistakes, allowing individuals to rape the globe and its people for profit without taking any responsibility. Money and its value don't exist any longer in the actual world, but are just digital amounts we agree to follow. This social money illusion is used to maintain the impoverishment of the many while sustaining the power of the global elite. The creation of something from nothing is an illusion made by magicians and should not enter the world of trade. A society that lives based on a resource it doesn't have is a society that's either waiting for a miracle or is aware of the disaster awaiting future generations. For the sake of creating a healthy monetary system that won't require endless resources to preserve itself, there needs to be a basic rule of existence. The rule is very simple: any person, entity, or group cannot use the resources he doesn't have in the real world. Such a rule promises control on the natural balance of things and will naturally prevent the abstract creation or concentration of power.

Governments are the guardians of our societies and population. Creating profit for those institutions is contradictory to their mission. The necessity of governments to create a surplus and profit on the account of its citizens to repay debts and their interest rates is absurd and creating an unproportionable burden on its citizens. Government should be bound to the same rules of existence as its individuals. Indeed, there are cases in which more resources will benefit the population in the short-term, but the long-term consequences of such actions to future generations aren't worth making the short-term marginally easier for us.

Many will argue that without today's system of government loans, the world as we know it today wouldn't be possible. To be quite honest, the situation of the economy and its government in 2017 is unconstructive to its population. We see this in the rates of unemployment, the economic crisis of the last 20 years, and in the high tax rates paid by citizens for the sake of paying the debts of previous generations and the unnecessary risks taken by private banks and business capitalists. Business is a field of economics; government is a field of management and philosophy. Government and economy do interact, as maintaining an economy is based partly on the belief of the investor in the power of the local government to maintain stability. Such a connection is a one-way direction connection and shouldn't cross to the other side, just as the courts of justice are parallel to government and economics but shouldn't cross each other. Such a structure is important and must be maintained. Governments should be concerned about benefitting their populations, just as the business man's concern should be creating capital (not profit) and the courts should be concerned about justice.

The idea of individual profit is dangerous and antisocial. The ideas surrounding its benefits are maintained by the social and educational systems of those days. The idea of profit breathes and screams destructive individualism. We'll discuss this subject in the next chapter. At this point, I will say that the idea of individualism is easy to reach for in a world that's too big to understand, a world run by new communication channels that we still don't master, and a world in which we've just come to understand that all humans are the same. The pursuit of individualistic dreams for profit reflects the root of our social problems. The pursuit of profit created the system we know today. The concentration of power and the incapability of the masses to maintain themselves is a direct consequence of this greed. The shortage of funds in our government system is a direct effect of the loan system that shouldn't concern the populous as it shouldn't be possible in the first place. Profit as a social order is a sickness, a sickness that passes to any human who touches it. It does not need a single language, religion, or location, as it is understood intuitively.

There's a difference between having a small personal surplus and being rich. As discussed above, the resources needed to maintain all humanity exist in nature. Some latest publications show that if we started spreading our resources based on human need and not based on profit, the general cost of production would diminish drastically, and we would avoid the majority of the waste creation. In a healthy global market, a structure of employment is needed. People that show more professional skills need to be paid more for their time. People should be able to accumulate small amounts of money. Import and export are healthy for local populations if done well, and the government raising taxes for specific projects is positive. To put it simply: the capitalist structure isn't bad, but it's not perfect either. The wave of protests against capitalism comes from ignorance and fear. All protests made by the populous against capitalism are, in fact, protests against profits and concentration of power. This misconception is a tool the profit seekers use as they turn the anger and frustration of the masses against a neutral system and not the individuals benefiting it. The rush after profit is antisocial and unproductive to any nation and humanity in the long run. The ability of a person to enslave another for profit they don't need should be illegal and monitored by all authorities. Understanding the problem is the first step towards finding a good solution.

We, as individuals, are creating the new world society. This new global era is not a myth or idea, but a reality we're headed toward and living every day. It's our responsibility to create a better world for future generations. If we stop telling ourselves that we're too small and too ignorant, we will start to understand the future is in our hands.

In the next chapter, we'll talk about the evolution of our societies social movements, and examine our options and possible processes for change. The actions taken are a consequence of our inner philosophy and the way we see life. Decisions based on practical ideas that promote the wellbeing of the future generation are good ideas that need to be executed even if they require to bear its consequences.

Let's us examine our options.

Chapter 3:

Society, values and social movements

Human nature

While discussing the ideas presented in the first two chapters with people, the subject of so-called "human nature" has come up many times as an opposition to those ideas. Based on Wikipedia's definition:

> *"Human nature refers to the distinguishing characteristics—including ways of thinking, feeling, and acting—which humans tend to have naturally. The questions of whether these are truly fixed characteristics, what these natural characteristics are, and what causes them are among the oldest and most important questions in philosophy and science. The concept of human nature is traditionally contrasted not only with unusual human characteristics, but also with characteristics derived from specific cultures and upbringings. The "nature versus nurture" debate is a well-known modern discussion about human nature. These questions have particularly important implications in economics, ethics, politics, and theology. This is partly because human nature can be regarded as both a source of norms of conduct or ways of life, as well as presenting obstacles or constraints on living a good life. The complex implications of such questions are also dealt with in art and literature, which often explore the question of what it is to be human."*

As we discussed in previous chapters, the "trap of words" is dominant when it comes to individual perspective. Questions regarding the nature of humans are fascinating, as they're questions with paradoxes containing many pre-existing assumptions. Without a doubt, an individual believing that humans are naturally bad or evil will have a hard time finding motivation to be part of a society, a city, or a country. Moreover, the mental implication of thinking in such terms affects how the individual judges themselves and can affect almost every aspect of their life.

Let's get into it. The idea that all human beings can be reduced to common traits is complicated and potentially far from words like nature. We can say that humans have common habits related to their education and life experience, which will be true. We can even say that some distant people can happen to share basic traits unrelated to their education, which doesn't prove anything when addressing questions regarding humanity as a whole. Such similarities are part of what we call basic human traits, which are easy to find if you're searching for them. But starting a sentence with "all humans are" is an impossible task, as there will always be exceptions. In all the modern social sciences (including psychology, economics, and sociology,) experiments based on statistics are valid proof, and in any study, there's always a few individuals that don't score like the majority of the people. This is the main reason we use statistics in the first place. The amount of existing variations in the human race is probably equal to the number of humans alive. We can also say that the number of similarities are endless depending on what one is searching for.

In general, looking at such an extreme metaphysical question (good and bad are two extremes) from a logical perspective will immediately reveal the problem. The usage of a sentence starting with "all the…" is, by itself, a dangerous presumption when addressing questions about humans. Based on the statistics available from the majority of research, such a sentence will be invalid immediately, as any research finds individuals the behaves differently. It's impossible to test and measure all humanity, which will always leave us a place to hope and speculate. Moreover, for every extreme case, we can find the opposite extreme as an example. There are true sentences about all humans. It will be safe to say all individuals have a specific, individual nature, that all humans have certain habits, and that there will always be an individual who reacts differently than another group. Many trials tried to find common universal traits, universal values, and universal tastes. None of them found any universal traits.

The unification of humans under one umbrella is healthy, as it's the key to cooperation. In the end, we do share common traits and common goals, exactly as we are different in others. The concentration on our common traits and goals is the first tool which can unify humans, while the concentration on our differences will undoubtedly create separation and fear.

Additionally, there are two problems that are completely ignored when discussing human nature. The first encompasses the assumptions related to concepts of the world and the term nature. The second relates to the misunderstanding of the terms good and bad.

Let's start with the first issue. What do we mean when we say human nature? Studying human history and development will quickly bring us to a conclusion that the idea of right and wrong changes with the time period and geographic location of the individuals in question. In some societies, values can stay or come and go, but this doesn't let us generalize anything. Humans, like the rest of the environment, are constantly evolving and changing over time. Trying to compare early humans to modern ones shows how traits have drastically evolved and changed over time. Those changes represent the physical, psychological, and social aspects of humanity. It's safe to assume that even if we all had a common nature at the beginning of our evolutionary process, it's so far from the point where we are today that we can assume those traits no longer exist. We've been evolving for at least 30,000 years, and have separated one from another, creating new habits and new natural dispositions. From the other side, if we search hard enough, we can find a certain nature that's survived. We can try to compare ourselves to animals that came from our same ancestors, like large apes. If someone put themselves next to one of our ape ancestors, they'd quickly identify similarities between humans and apes. Natural behavior like sleeping, eating, and social groups are necessary in nature, not just to humans. This logic exercise shouldn't make you think we have the same nature as our ape cousins, but rather to doubt the blind belief that we still share a certain nature. Humans are separate from other mammals and very unique. Humans are very special; our behavior is based on mental processes involving the projection of possible futures. Human nature is to think and imagine, which make it neither good or bad. Nature by itself defines everything that is happening realistically. Each object, animal and entity have its nature. as long as something exist it have a nature. it is obligatory. Based on this logic, we can say that all humans have their own nature. But, there's still no conclusion about a universal, common nature.

The second, and probably more important point, is the paradox used in the question of human nature regarding the issue of good and bad. Those traits are abstract measurements prescribed by humans that represent two extremes and require each other to exist. The majority of philosophers handling the question of human nature do so by asking if humans are good or bad. This question is not only relative, but also based on terms that change based on culture and time. Good is a relative term, with its opposite called bad. Before even tackling this issue, it's easy to understand the basic problem when addressing such questions. To make it easy, for a person to be good, one must be bad next to him. It's required when using comparative terms. In reality, if all people are good or all people are bad, they are neither as they will be only people. When it comes to humans and evolution in general, it's safe to say that an observation of specific individuals in a certain period will never hold for too long, as humans change and evolve. Extremes like good and bad are used to understand the framework and not the individuals in it. Moreover, as good and bad are not absolute, comparable units, it's impossible to use them as anchors without giving a specific definition before starting the comparison.

To understand this point better, let's take a case in which using absolute extremes is possible. We can use black and white as extremes for understanding the variety of colors, as colors are comparing themselves to black and white. One doesn't need to see white to identify a black color, as black can stand by itself. From the other side, good is extremely relative. In many cases, good is a measurement used by humans to express a trait compared to a similar, previous experience. For example, a good grade can be relative to an absolute standard, relative to the grades other people received, relative to the grades one achieved on previous exams, or relative to the grades an individual thought they received. A good kid, good chair, good day, and good weather are all relative to one of the options mentioned above. Additionally, every outcome that *isn't* 'good,' may not be 'bad' either. There's a range of realities which are part of a segment that is neither good nor bad. The vocabulary used to express those options varies between languages and cultures. In English, terms like ok, fine, and acceptable are all part of this spectrum.

When it comes to humans and their nature, the usage of good and bad can be done in two ways: by comparison to another human or to a fixed standard. If we use the first technique, the exercise will be absurd, as it requires a bad human to have a good human, which will bring us to the conclusion that there are all kinds of people. The other technique is even more absurd. Since the standard of good and bad have to be fixed up front, the fact that right and wrong change based on time and location will bring the criteria to be undefinable in the first place.

Even in one time period, norms regarding good and bad are different even based only on location. For example, in some cultures, a good person does what he believes is good and right, while in another culture, that behavior is seen as chaotic and anti-social. After all, it's a very self-concentrated and unpredictable behavior. Another example is the idea of failure. In the US and other countries around the world, failure is seen as a good thing because we can learn from failure. But in many European countries, failure is seen as bad and something to be ashamed of.

Humans are what they are, meaning they're similar in some moments and traits and different in others. We can even say that all humans are similar and different from one another in certain moments and periods. Occupying ourselves with the wrong questions can bring us bad conclusions. The concept of human nature in terms of good and bad is a horrible way to lose faith in ourselves and the world around us. In reality, humans are good in certain moments and bad in others.

To put it simply, following years of social evolution and physical separation between humans over the globe, it's safe to say that human nature evolves based on their surroundings and that humans hold beliefs taught through education and society. Humans will naturally follow a certain path of behavior based on their education and their life experiences.

As we are social animals acting based on our own predictions (made in one individual's mind and there alone), the importance of holding the right set of beliefs is crucial for building a society. A famous saying in psychology coined by Abraham Kaplan and later on quoted by Abraham Maslow in 1966 is called "the law of instruments." In his quote, he said, "I suppose it is tempting, If the only tool you have is a hammer, to treat everything as it were nails."

People who believe humans are naturally bad will find evidence everywhere, just as someone who believes everyone is good will find as much proof. When the two extremes of a philosophical argument are proven to be true, we can conclude that the reality is somewhere in the middle. What, then, is the solution for our question of human nature? To start, we can conclude that we don't possess a common nature to the point of generalizing humanity. We all share some traits which are beyond our control, but those traits also exist in other mammals, which makes them a natural behavior of mammals and not humans. We can also safely assume that the majority of the humans have some common traits that guide them. Humans build their beliefs mainly based on their education, societies, and personal perspective. The use of terms like 'human nature' is dangerous and misleading as it fixes a set of beliefs in the individual's mind that represents a segment of reality. Moreover, this categorization of humanity creates an assumption that impose ignorance on individuals when looking in on themselves, their neighbors, and the world.

Throughout history, we can find acts that stem selfishness and self-interest. The interesting thing about those cases is that they normally refer to a minority of individuals and not society as a whole. Humans are unpredictable and don't have the capacity to predict the behavior others. A moment of self-reflection will reveal moments and actions in an individual's life that surprise them, and moments in which their closest friends' actions surprise them. This doesn't mean that we don't possess general guidelines in our lives. It just means that sometimes, we act based on different values. In the end, life is very dynamic and constantly changing.

There will always be a minority who act against the "common good." These people hold a different set of beliefs, and should be always considered as such. As we are entering a new "global era," it's important to understand that we are as similar as we are different. As we'll see in this chapter, the unification of humanity under one sets of values isn't required for the creation a better world. Instead, we must accept humans regardless of their differences and similarities, their belief in the majority of humans create a better future, and their willingness to oppress and ignore the minorities that try to separate us with violence and fear. We're all part of this planet, and we're all sometimes good and sometimes bad. The majority of people on this planet prefer to live peacefully in their homes and raise families while belonging to a constructive society, knowing they're part of something bigger than themselves. We are all indeed part of something bigger than ourselves; it is called humanity. For better or worse, this is what we have. We can choose to actively be part of it or ignore it, living in our small isolated islands that we call our life. Doing so won't change the fact that we're all in it together, and only together will we manage to create a better future for ourselves, our kids, and our planet.

Strong Societies Require Strong Individuals

Society is a group of people who interact with each other persistently, or a large social grouping sharing the same geographical territory, typically but not necessarily subject to the same political authority and dominant cultural expectations.

Society is the foundation that allows for the creation and maintenance of a government. Throughout history, ruling parties have varied in their size, form, and policy. Additionally, common interest is the foundation of any group, pack, or society, as its fundamental purpose is to promote self-interest in the form of large-scale cooperation. We can easily agree that without benefitting from joining a group, no individual will make the effort of creating or maintaining one in the first place. Based on this assumption, we can hope that in case no common interest will serve the individuals in society, a natural need for change will grow in the society, and bring individuals to act. Unfortunately, as we can see, even if the majority of the population is aware that their interests are not served, a lack of alternatives makes the population accept the malfunction of their own societies, by maintaining a passive and self-concentrated way of life.

As all social systems are the creation of humans and for their benefit, it would be absurd to assume that a system can be stronger than a human without the full agreement and cooperation of individuals in the first place. This point is very important, but many people forget it. A society can exist without a government, but a government cannot exist without a society. Following decades of social oppression and missteps, this basic rule, which should balance our societies, has been replaced by tyranny, fear, and separation. Without a doubt, the extreme changes in the world in the last 500 years have contributed to this mentality.

Another reason individuals may feel weak in front of their government is the size of the society itself. The creation of mega cities is new, at least compared to how long humans have existed. The migration to cities and the creation of mega cities, which became mega countries, is a development of the last 200 years of our history. In small communities and even in moderately-sized cities, a social cycle exists in which everybody knows each other to a certain degree. Even if there is no direct connection, a second or third degree of connection is enough to create a feeling of control. For example, if I do not know a person, but he is a friend of a friend, our willingness to cooperate will be immediate as we believe we share a connection. The creation of mega populations and mega countries has left individuals feeling lost in the stream of difference and loneliness. This feeling is created by individuals feeling they don't know the majority of people surrounding them and do not have the capacity to affect them. In this situation, an individual's belief that they can practically affect their society diminishes drastically as the society becomes an abstract term and not a practical one.

As the population grows, this feeling grows in each person. The creation of mega nations in the last 200 years has changed the structure and ideas standing behind our societies, which changed our cities and the people in them. In this reality, mobs and self-interested rich parties can easily take control of the population because they're accessible and weak.

Societies are no longer built on the foundation of the old societies. Humanity has practiced social cooperation the same way for thousands of years without any drastic change. Hierarchies of the elite have been replaced by new ones and empires have fallen and been replaced by the arrival of a new one. In old-style empires, the social structure of cities stayed in many ways the same regardless of the changing empire. In many cases, the empire itself didn't handle the day-to-day activities of its cities and didn't promote the creation of mega societies. The Industrial Revolution, followed by the technological evolution of the last 150 years, has created a reality so different for the individual's day-to-day life, that any attempt to build a society or economy based on the ancient structure and philosophy can only lead to the destruction of the society itself. The cause for the creation of our societies and the tools used to maintain the old societies and economies aren't relevant to the current system nor to the needs of today's population. Factories have changed available occupations, bringing an influx of migrants to cities while the creation of bureaucratic employment changed the requirement of the employment itself. The creation of mega cities started with the Industrial Revolution, but evolved drastically only after the creation of the bureaucratic system dating less than 100 years.

As life became more complicated and our goals started to change, we got so used to the idea of being ruled that we forgot to ask ourselves the primary purpose and role of the system itself. The creation of a single, powerful man holding concentrated power has evolved with creation of societies. In a society of 1,000 people, there is no need for a concentration of power as long as all the individuals in it are loyal to the same values and principles, while living in full respect to those values and to the people around. Natural courses of humanity have brought different empires to rise and fall, as the need of the people stopped being served by their rulers and became hostile to the prosperity of the masses.

Following the mass expansion of monotheistic religions across the globe over at least 2,000 years—including the mass expansion of Christianity and Islam—the obedience to authority and fear of an omnipotent entity became the status quo. With time and repetition, this system became a norm around the globe. Such a long period lived this way, brought the society to become preoccupied with the leaders of their systems instead of the systems themselves. This way of thinking is a deceptive separation created by individual fanatics for the sake of control.

In the 21st century, individuals in Western society have adopted a dichotomic philosophy which is imposed by the media and government. In a time of crisis, the government will take a position of "with us or against us." This tool of fear and extremism is the basic way humans are controlled by the capitalistic system, just like any other form of tyranny. This dichotomy promotes social acceptance of a structure in which there are only two kinds of people: capitalist and laborer, good or bad, progress or destruction. This way of thinking has become a norm accepted by individuals, repeated on a normal daily basis.

The capitalist evolution in the Western market has drastically changed the way its subjects perceive their government, their time, their society and their purpose in life. The stronger the foundation of capitalism in the life of a society, the more the individuals will develop a self-concentrated personality which can be manipulated by fear of the 'other' and excitement of profit. Such a self-doctrine separates the individual from their society, disconnects them from their surroundings, and makes them develop a habit of obedience and fear over time.

The merging of the economic market with the government has made the controller of the economy more powerful than the governments and citizens. The ability of a government to engage itself on the economic stage by taking loans is an anti-social system, as it's based on a fluctuating currency that represents nothing but itself. Such a decision has created our current reality, one in which our governments are pushed to engage in the loan path for the sake of the government's survival. This path will inevitably collapse while taking the majority of its citizens with it. This process will be reflected in the impoverishment and misery of the population, while allowing the elite to survive and levitate above the economy itself. The massive loans taken by governments to cover their depths is a spiral of the inability to find a better solution. As the loans are taken mainly to cover interest rates and not to repay the loans, a philosophy of "let's solve the problem tomorrow, tomorrow" has been created. This reality leads to the devaluation of the time of the individual and their property, security, and self-image.

In 2017, the governments in Western society serves as singular entities that see everything, judge without a possibility to argue, and punish citizens as they please, while rewarding their subjects for following their wishes blindly. It is true to say that the law and court houses exists. Nevertheless, their occupation is concentrated in a small amount of cases. In the daily life of a westerner, the local police and the enforcement entity are the judges and the executioner of the law. In many cases, the economical capacity of an individual will determine the result of its judgment and not the justice principal. Over time, when many generations are educated in this reality, individuals will comply with the government for maintenance of society and personal safety.

As society is a living and evolving organism, there's no wrong way to evolve as long as the capacity to change exists. Nassim Nicholas Taleb describes a theory of antifragility in his wonderful book *Antifragility*, beautifully explaining the idea of inevitable change and the West's fear of new possibilities. The idea of antifragility dictates that change in life is inevitable and should be seen as a constant to look forward to, as it brings new opportunity. A person or organization that tries to preserve the current reality will inevitably collapse. The modern economic and political doctrine is based on a trial to maintain its existence and to fear change. A society that doesn't understand the necessity of change and the opportunities that it brings is a regressive society that will make the process of change harder for itself.

The evolution of our governing system has brought many peoples to see subjects like economy and government as complex topics that should be avoided. Such a mentality is anti-social, and those subjects are not only relevant to every day to day aspect of society. But, they're also the main tool used to create better societies and creates progress. Weak and confused individuals create weak societies. The willingness and ability of individuals to understand and engage in social activities that create change are the keys for creating strong societies.

The Technological Evolution and its Implications

The unification of humans under a globalized system is a natural process evolving rapidly in our generation. The implication and inventions following the technological revolution aren't complete. Good tools can be used badly in the process of understanding the power of those tools. These days, people approach the majority of novelties with little skepticism, which turns to over-assuming the positives of the new tools.

Every revolution requires adaptation. When it comes to changes like the internet, smart phones, and other tools recently developed, it's safe to say that a period of extreme usage will be necessary before understanding the right use for these technologies. This process also occurred after the Industrial Revolution. In the early days of the Industrial Revolution, the overuse of machines and overwork of people was disastrous until humans understood the effects of overusing those tools and created laws to govern their usage. The technological revolution is, by far, the most remarkable tool for creating a global world, but it's important to understand how to use new technology and, more importantly, how not to use it.

The accessibility of information in a fraction of a second and the communication of the individuals with their society without the need of knowledge or physical movement, has fundamentally changed the needs of Western society. The more connected a person is to their society by indirect means of communication, the lonelier they will become. When an individual spends most of their time closed in their home, they create a cage for themselves, and this separation is antisocial. An individual born in a metropolis is not only living as a lion born in a cage, but is also convinced it's the best way of living without understanding the alternatives. In this reality, social growth is minimal, as a society requires its people to actively exist for growth. When a society gives the individual an unrealistic, detached feeling of unity and community while sitting in their home, the individual's capability of understanding what right and wrong changes. In this case, right and wrong will be dictated by the media, without any serious objection from the individuals. As we can observe in our society today, most people don't know what's good for themselves, but are confident in their own opinion when it comes to their personal beliefs about what's good for others. If a society degenerates to living individuals living in their golden cages, humans will progressively forget that their greatest strength is to create.

The technological revolution as a tool of mass control and isolation of individuals has brought Western society to a new era unlike anything we've seen before. We're a population living with a feeling that something is wrong, while we're busy telling ourselves that everything is under control and that we have freedom. The capability of the individual to notice that the system is malfunctioning didn't vanish, but the feeling of responsibility as part of society and the will to fight for a better society no longer exists. The need for a populous that acts when they suffer injustice is fundamental for progress and democracy.

As our friends, money, and achievements become immaterial, and as technology rules our lives, our ability to distinguish between what's real and not becomes blurred. The majority of the people living in the West are terrorized by events happening far away, controlled by people they never actually met, dreaming about places they've never seen, and trying to look and sound like people they've never met. The use of new technology is one of the tools available for our unification. Used in the wrong way, this tool can become our controller. The need for a life in the physical world is essential for maintaining good societies with healthy individuals. It's not a system that should tell us what to do or how to do it. It's us, as a community, that should support each other and keep each other on a healthy and progressive path. As the world is controlled by a small elite doing everything in its power to isolate us for the sake of controlling us, we must understand the danger and benefits of the technological revolution to shape our future. A good standard can be fixed, the "standard of reality." Such a standard can be seeing as followed - If the use of technological tools promotes practical physical achievements that can be seen and measured in real life, those tools are used well. In case the achievements stay in the domain of the immaterial world, the use of the tool is unhealthy and destructive.

Technology brought humanity tools that changed every aspect of human life. Without any doubt, it's an additional stage in our communication evolution. Like any other tools invented by humans, these are good as long as they serve us and become a danger when they become a necessity to our survival.

The path we're walking is clear. It follows a plan made by people that have the knowledge, power, and funds for massive execution. The violence of today is a tool to make individuals terrified and terrorized in their own homes. Violence is one of the tools of the ancient world, as separation, tyranny, capitalism, and egoism ruled all societies. These aren't required in a world in which we understand we're all part of the same global society.

Individualism

The ability of the masses to successfully cooperate is based on the willingness of individuals to cooperate and believe in the movement. The platform of communication, the knowledge available to the mass market, and our natural capacity for creation are the fundamental tools needed to create a necessary change. The knowledge of individuals regarding the history of their people and the history of humanity is essential to creating a clear identity. By understanding history, one can learn not only what we have tried to do, but also what we have never been. In the way the history is taught these days, the information given in formal institutions concentrates on war and disasters of others while prizing our own victories. History is not concentrated in the temporary success of one group or another, but it's a process in which humanity evolved out of trial and error.

Thanks to new technology, we can learn and share information internationally, allowing us to observe the evolution of humanity from all over the world as one history. Preaching history out of a philosophy of fear and separation will inevitably create a general feeling of terror and misery. Learning history in such a way can only send a general message regarding our history, it is a matter of time until someone will come to take our place. With such a set of beliefs, general cooperation is, without a doubt, impossible. Only by seeing human history as a process of trial and error will individuals possess the tools of knowledge and freedom, which are essential for creating a better future.

The more awareness we have regarding our existence and our history, the closer we get to the understanding that peace and prosperity are possible by sacrificing the tyranny of the few and profit. This will create a better future for all. The need for power is no longer created out of a shortage of resources, ignorance regarding our similarities, and our wish for peace and happiness. An individual without a clear understanding of human history lacks the tools necessary to understand where they come from, which makes it impossible to understand where they are now. This lack of understanding will inevitably extinguish the individual's capacity to understand where they would like to go in the future.

Individuals in such a reality will have a natural tendency to follow the system imposed on them and focus on themselves. Two kinds of the self-concentration exist. They are "constructive individualism" and "destructive individualism." It is important to understand the difference between the both, as one is the key for a strong society and the second is one of the causes for its destruction. Wikipedia defines individualism as:

> "Individualism is the moral stance, political philosophy, ideology, or social outlook that emphasizes the moral worth of the individual. Individualists promote the exercise of one's goals and desires, they value independence and self-reliance, and they advocate that the interests of the individual take precedence over the state or a social group. They oppose external interference upon one's own interests by society or institutions such as the government. Individualism is often defined in contrast to totalitarianism, collectivism, authoritarianism, communitarianism, tribalism, and more corporate social forms, which is, in many cases, championed by an antisocial interest group, Individualism makes the individual its focus and so starts "with the fundamental premise that the human individual is of primary importance in the struggle for liberation." Classical liberalism, existentialism, and anarchism are examples of movements that take the human individual as a central unit

of analysis. Individualism thus involves "the right of the individual to freedom and self-realization."

To fully understand the fundamental implication of individualism, it's important to establish a few basic ideas. First, in each person's life, the specific individual is the center of their own life. This is an important point that is easy to prove. Observing any living thing, it can be said that its perspective is always cycling around its own existence, which is, in many cases, a limitation or a starting point. There is nothing wrong with that. Only by understanding this principle can a person fully understand themselves, their position in their environment, and society. In a society searching for equality and freedom, individuals must understand who they are and their strengths for the system to function properly. Such individualism is healthy and should be adopted by any society to evolve and flourish. It's easy to understand how this philosophy creates some difficulties when it comes to maintaining a social order that doesn't benefit the individual. This doesn't make the individual's behavior problematic, but the system itself. The fear individuals feel regarding this idea is normally based on beliefs like "humans are naturally bad," or just from needing to control others. In reality, if individuals start taking care of themselves and believe in their individual capacity, they will start to take care of their society and believe in their ability to change it.

Based on this idea we can define constructive individualism as, "self-aware behavior in which an individual accepts and understands themselves their abilities and limitations, and takes active part their society based on the principal that dictates that a strong society requires strong individuals."

From the other side, the individualism preached these days is very far from this concept. It's an individualism based on the need to satisfy one's wishes and goals while ignoring the needs of society. This destructive individual can be defined as, "self-concentration and the pursuit of personal ambition, while ignoring the needs and nature of the society." The symptoms of such a philosophy are clear and will inevitably bring individuals to over-consume and develop a feeling of omnipotence, while criticizing anything that's different from what they have. The emptiness that evolves over time will bring individuals to fear what they do not understand, while ignoring clear signs of self and social destruction.

Trying to explain this concept to a kid is very hard as it doesn't make sense in the first place. Kids hold a constructive individualism as they are mainly aware of their perspective and naturally try to be an active part of their surroundings. Alas, a large part of adults living in the Western world not only hold values of destructive individualism, but also defend those standards proudly when discussing the subject.

Looking at our history, such self-concentrated, destructive individualism was held mainly by a small group of riches in power living by privilege, maintained by the impoverishment and enslavement of the rest of the population. The evolution of such a consciousness in the masses is new. It evolved in the West only in the last 70 years. Many factors affected this trend and supported it during its spread. The rise of the middle class following the development of democracies, the beginning of cheap manufacture in far countries, the rise of the standard of living, and the adaptation of consumerism are only a few factors that pushed such negative behavior. Retrospectively, it's hard to conclude if the spread of the destructive individualism was a cause or an effect. The only thing we can say with certainty is that in 2017, the socially detached, self-concentrated, wasteful, and violent way of life became a new standard that is held and even praised by many.

Two other changes left a vacuum in the human mind that needed to be filled, which helped in the rise of such a social standard. The first is the fall of nationalism in the second half of the 20th century, and the second is the lack of religious belief of the new generation. The fall of nationalism and the lack of belief in a demanding, controlling god has created a need for answers and causes for social motivation. The study of nationalism and monotheism will show that those concepts are, first of all, social. Nationalism, by definition, is a social concept as it concentrates on the unification, and many times supremacy, of a specific nation. The monotheistic religions demand a lot from any individual follower, but nevertheless, the amount of social duties and activities required instantly create a social order for its followers. Following the fall of those two concepts, individuals need an alternative path for their private lives and their role in society.

The idea that one controls their own fate without the need for abstract gods and nations has been practiced for many years by Hindus, while preserving a relatively peaceful social structure and a constructive system. It's not a way of life preached by the West, but that doesn't make it less relevant or less socially productive in the big picture of humanity. For an individual born and raised in the West, the knowledge and traditions of the East are a mystery that, without a lot of self-motivation, will stay in the realm of mysticism and polytheistic religions.

Looking at it honestly, it's easy to see how following the fall of nationalism and monotheism, the dedication to money and self-interest are more acceptable concepts for Westerners, as they're similar traits to the old concepts. The pursuit of profit, control, and domination was a big part of the European-American culture to start with, as they were the natural way of life in Europe for hundreds of years. Looking at the evolution of individualism, it can be said that nationalism and monotheistic religions were the pole holding the social values of individuals in the Western world. Without those two, all that's left from the rise of the Western empire is greed, power, and domination, based on ignorance, fear, and separation.

Without any doubt, some positive and constructive social values have remained in small and medium communities.

Individuals raised in small and medium communities, detached from the media and aggressive social lifestyle, still hold many positive social values not found in big cities. The creation of mega cities, the evolution of the media, and the integration of the capitalist scheme has left individuals with few tools to understand and hold social values. After all, life in the big cities in the West has been described by many as a concrete jungle, which has its own rules and values.

In the last 50 years, the way the world is working changed drastically and became more complex and demanding. Such reality pushes individuals to feel small and incapable as the systems become abstract and violent. The rise of destructive individualism is exactly the separative philosophy needed for the reign of tyranny. We can see that many people living in big cities don't know or care about their neighbors, are concerned about and afraid of another ethnic groups around them, and see the government as a faraway entity concentrated on promoting its own self-interest at the cost of the wellbeing of its subjects.

The education and evolution of a few generations under such a reality has brought many to believe that the best way to handle reality is to concentrate on self-promotion and security of specific individuals while concentrating on small and local ways to obtain money. The overconsumption, social status achieved by materialism, and the need of many for a faraway vacation are all symptoms of a dying social structure. It's one thing to work hard and to save money for hard days, and another to work hard for the sake of buying things one doesn't need for social acceptance. In such a society, the willingness and capacity of individuals to create constructive and active social movement is small to non-existent.

Moreover, if a person needs to continue to work only for the sake of maintaining a shelter and obtaining food, it's safe to say that the individual is part of "the 21st century Western slavery." After all, if the only way an individual can survive is to enter the working cycle, and the working cycle is built in a way that promises the worker will never have enough for their basic needs. By any standard, it can be called slavery. The fact that a person can chose his occupation in the system do not make it less of the "slavery system." It's not surprising that in such a slavery system, each person will be for themselves and values as force, destructive individualism, and violence will be held by many. The key for social structure is communication and trust. The lack of one of them or both will inevitably push individuals to become self-concentrated and paranoid, a reality that is unhealthy for any individual and antisocial in any case.

It's important to make the separation between constructive and destructive individualism. A deep understanding of the concept of individualism and its role in society will bring us to discover how verbally close the two terms are, while practically representing extremes. A strong society requires strong individuals who understand their place, roles, and capacity in an active society. Without such individuals, the society will degenerate to become a blind herd led by any entity that presents enough power and consistency. A society without strong and active individuals won't have the capacity to evaluate and change its governing system and its norms as needed, which is contradictory to some basic presumptions in a society that tries to be free and democratic.

From the other side, destructive individualism is probably one of the main tools needed to weaken a society and bring its individuals to lose their tools normally used to maintain autonomy and power in a democratic society. Self-concentrated, over-materialistic individuals who are mainly preoccupied by their social acceptance, exhibit anti-social behavior patterns. An individual who sees social isolation as the end of everything they value and would rather live as a slave to a system than die a free master of their own existence will become the engine of the slavery of a social system.

Many will say that the individuals in the Western world are

living today better than kings 300 years ago. That's probably true if measured in terms of technological development, which prove that as a species, we evolve drastically and not that we are less slaves than we used to be. In terms of free time, basic needs, and self-autonomy in front of our government, not only are we not evolving, but we're regressing. All those factors are essential for maintaining the power of the rich elite. It secures the functional continuation of the mechanism in future years. In case of any trial of change, the capacity of the media to expose individuals to threat and extreme violence promises the fear and obedience of the masses. It's not the first time in history that an elite group is enslaving populations for the sake of their own power and profit, but it's probably the first time that so many individuals are busy telling themselves that this is the best way to live. As mentioned above, any social movement requires motivated self-aware individuals for its success. The separation, fear, and ignorance of the majority of the Western civilization is not only maintaining the tyranny of profit and the enslavement of themselves, but is also the main reason no social change is possible. The concentration and importance individuals put in the small details of their own lives has become the curse of society, as it makes them blind to their surrounding and society.

The Chronicle of Social Change

As long as the elite maintain a fair feeling with their subjects regarding standard of living, the law of common interest will create a society in which the exploitation of the many is accepted for the sake of personal gain. Looking at history, we can see this balance requires a unique kind of elite that understand the importance of this balance. In reality, regardless of which society we decide to look at during history, there has always been a small group in charge of ruling and a bigger group being ruled. Nevertheless, it's always a matter of time until the balance between those groups breaks and requires a social change. As nothing stays constant, it is clear that with time, one of the groups will require more than it required previously for the sake of its survival, which will create an immediate shortage for the other. The studies of such moments in history hold the keys to the understanding of the nature of our social changes.

For any social movement to be launched, a general feeling of unfairness has been created in one of the groups, which requires the termination of the existing system. There are two options for terminating the existing system:

- A movement created by the population itself against the system, which destroys the existing system and creates a new system in their image
- Self-destruction by the elite in power

In many cases, the self-destruction of the system by the elite and its reconstruction will emerge when the elite can no longer exploit the masses and maintain power.

When the system is destroyed by the elite, as can be seen in the West today, the change and construction of the new system will be controlled and maintained by the few for their own benefit. In these cases, it can be assumed that the new system will fundamentally erect itself on the same principals. A system based on the exploitation of the many for the creation of additional power will create a cycle of impoverishment and enslavement of the many for the wealth of the few. This endless cycle is contradictory to the nature of the creation of a society, as it's a cycle that doesn't benefit the majority of its people.

We can see examples of this cycle in Western history in the years 80-1200 AD. It is a period considered the "dark age of Europe," as the domination by the Catholic church maintained itself with different leaders and countries for the sake of the elite.

Other examples are the enslavement of the African people in the early United States, in the peasants of pre-revolutionary Russia, and in today's modern enslavement of the masses in the European community.

The tools of violence and intimidation are fascinating when it comes to maintaining power. Unfortunately, we will not discuss this subject, as it will take us away from the purpose of this book. It is possible to find many political and historical books describing and discussing those matters, including *The Shock Doctrine* by Naomy Klein and *Wage of Rebellion* by Chris Hedges.

Violence and intimidation are easy to create and effective in maintaining power. Research shows that to create constant fear in an individual's mind, a disproportionate violence must be used first, followed by its unpredictable repetition while emphasizing a clear understanding of the outcomes.

One of the founders of cognitive Psychology, Martin Seligman, discovered a general behavior called "learned helplessness" in the year 1967. Learned helplessness is a behavior typical to animals that have endured repeated painful or otherwise aversive stimuli in which the animal is unable to escape or avoid. After such repetition, the person or animal will often fail to learn and practice ways of escape or avoidance in new situations, where such behavior would be effective and needed. In other words, a person exposed to various direct or indirect terror and intimidation, while learning that it is impossible to prevent or effect the situations, will unconsciously believe they have lost control, so they will give up trying to fight or change the situation. Learned helplessness theory is the view that clinical depression and related mental illnesses may result from such real or perceived absence of control over the outcome of a situation.

This tool used by the elite to deprive and control the many is not only seen in the unproportionable militant violence inside and outside of a country. This tool takes shape as a social status when different enforcement groups in the society create physical learned helplessness as the fear of faceless violence of the system is unpredictable and a violence become a habit.

The violence and intimidation can be seen in many other fields in which the individual will gradually lose their belief in their capacity to make a change in their country, city, community, and in themselves. David Graeber wrote a book called *The Utopia of Rules: On Technology, Stupidity and the Secret Joys of Bureaucracy* which discusses the evolution of the bureaucratic system in the 21st century and its effect on the individual and society. The creation of a complicated, changing bureaucratic system doesn't benefit its citizens and creates a system in which the individuals become lost in a system that they fear, dislike, and don't understand.

By creating a system maintained by force, terror, isolation of the individual, and their enslavement to the system, inevitably with the time a need to increase the amount of violence and intimidation will grow as a necessity to the system itself will requiring more resources. Following this conclusion, it is easy to create a simple tool to observe which society is in this cycle. If the amount of physical enforcement by the government is increasing with time, while diminishing the capacity of the individual to maintain a better way of life, the system is an antisocial system ruled by the elite and maintained by the enslavement of the many. A society living in such a system is doomed to have an unstable government, unproductive society, a fluctuating economy, and the domination of an exterior force to conquer or swallow the society as a whole as it will eventually be drained of its resources.

Throughout history, social systems that increasingly disserve the masses are inevitably demolished and destroyed by an active population. The amount of exploitation and number of switches of the socially destructive system needed to rally the populous vary based on the power of the local ruling class and the mentality of the local subjects. In most of the cases, the more time it takes for the populous to raise against their oppressive rulers, the less likely they are to have the means and power to bring to a countable and constructive change.

Active populations have two options to demolish the current system. We will group the movements as a "constructive movement" and a "depressing movement" by the populous. The distinction is simple and based on the fundamental idea of why the destruction must occur and how it is done. The concept of individuals acting out of rage or anger is known and can be observed as an instinctive act, based on momentary impulses of violence and unplanned action. Such movements may randomly yield positive results, but assuming that there is a lesson to learn from it, it's similar to claiming that a person believing that there is a connection between their random appearance in a bar is the reason for hearing a specific song. An important assumption at this point is the fact that by doing random acts in a random moment, random positive results will appear, doesn't mean that it's a good course of action. From the other side, maintaining a good, constant philosophy of action can bring in the process unwanted outcome. It doesn't change the fact that by practicing a certain philosophy of life constantly, various results will appear, which, if done right, will bring the outcome needed.

It can be better understood in the following example. If a wall of bricks is standing still and people randomly are passing and hitting the wall, at a certain point, the hit of a random person will break the wall. The only real conclusion that can be taken out of this experience is not that the individual in question has an enormous power or an unseen purpose, but that a wall hit repeatedly will eventually break. From the other side, hitting a wall of bricks with a big hammer will, in most of cases, break the wall in the first hit. A specific example in which the hit with the hammer will not brake the wall will not prove in any case that the hammer is not a good solution. In this case, other parameter can affect the failure of the specific hit, which doesn't make the tool less useful.

Going back to our population, a depressive movement is, in most cases, a violent and random act that starts as frustration and hated directed to an abstract entity. Normally fueled by mobs and extremists to promote their agendas, these movements concentrate on the immediate benefits of the act itself. Most of these movements finish with an extreme act of violence against the population itself by the ruling elite, or by the creation of a "new system" ruled by mobs. For the majority of the population, the act of violence by the government or the new ruling mob makes no difference, as they look and feel the same. Both are an oppressive act by the ruling elite on its population. The re-creation of a system by the mob is a re-creation that is no different from the system destroyed. Those mobs and extremists have nothing to lose by creating such a movement, as they'll benefit from the chaos created by the movement or finish as leaders of the new system. It is a win-win situation for them. In any case, possible gains compared to the potential losses is unproportionable and indeed attractive for any mob groups.

Those movements that normally start following a violent act by the ruling elite develop as acts of rage and ignorance, as they don't attack the actual social problem that requires a controlled change by removing the social virus while maintaining the survival of the society. In most cases, the movement concentrated on specific, temporary events for the general destruction of the whole system will pursue destruction for the sake of destruction. In most of those depressive movements, the leaders are normally local mobs and self-interested people acting mainly out of interest for power and profit. Those individuals or organizations use the general frustration and confusion of the masses for pure destruction and chaos

As the power and the tools of the local ruling elite are normally violent, the superiority of the ruling elite is certain in case of a violent encounter. The elite that hold power through violence are not only masters of those tools, but are also investing in upgrades of those tools to maintain power. It is easy to understand how an uprising by the populous based on tools of violence is the weakest attack possible as it's the field of domination for the elite. The lack of understanding regarding this point is, by itself, a tool of the elite. Moreover, revolting through violence will serve the elite, as they require a demonstration of power once in a while for the sake of maintaining their status. In other words, the creation of a violent movement against a government will benefit the ruling elite itself if the movement fails to dismantle the system. Using violence against the ruling elite can be compared to an unprofessional person believing that they will be able to defeat a professional in their field, just because they think it's the right thing to do. As we discussed earlier, a violent revolt can randomly be successful, which doesn't allow us to arrive to any conclusion except the fact that even professional people can make mistakes.

Depressive movements got their name based on the consequences of the movement itself. As we mentioned previously, when a social movement is violent, there are three possible outcomes. Two involve complete destruction of the system, and one involves the failure of the movement. In case the movement fails due to the use of extreme violence by the government or the failed maintenance of the violent movement itself by the masses, the oppression of the society is inevitable both mentally and physically. Such a failure will undoubtedly increase the power of the local ruling elite, will decrease the individual's confidence and belief in their ability to control themselves, and an economic burden will be imposed on the individuals for the reconstruction needed following the destruction. The failure of a movement thanks to an un-proportional act of violence increases the power of the ruling elite in all the cases.

The spirit of the individuals that engage themselves as an active part of their society in the revolt will not only abuse their will of active participation, but will adopt a feeling of learned helplessness that will isolate and depress their mentality. In case of a few failures of violent movements, the individual will no longer be open to new, positive alternatives. In case a population fails to revolt, not only will the individuals in it be smashed and terrorized by their own government, but the cost of the reconstruction will be so high and aggressive that it will strengthen the ruling elite.

If a violent movement does destroy the system, there are two possible long-term outcomes. In many cases, the masses don't usually understand the process of destruction or lack the knowledge and understanding of successful re-construction. This is seen in many anti-governmental movements; the majority of the populous involved is well aware of what they don't like about the current system, and have an abstract idea of how they'd would like their new life to look, but don't possess the knowledge and understanding of what to do, how to do it, and the actual cost. As the movement itself has been pushed and fueled by self-interested mobs and extremists, the first possible outcome is the creation of a new government in the shape of the mob and the extremists themselves. The creation of a new system by a small group of self-interested people is no different than the previous system, which is fundamentally contradictory to the primary idea of the masses uprising. In such a reality, the outcome's effect on the majority of the individuals won't be very different if the movement failed instead. Individuals will not only develop learned helplessness regarding their power and influence on their social system, but they'll feel all political movements lack efficiency and purpose.

The second possible outcome of a successful movement created by local mobs and extremists is the lack of leadership in the new system. This will make it impossible to reconstruct a social system. In this case, a period of chaos and violence will be created, promoted and pushed by the people controlling the natural resources and the largest quantity of armies and guns. In this case, the individual's standard of living and comfort will decrease, which will inevitably leave citizens with a sense of failure. In this case, the individual will not only learn that they don't have the power to shape their social system, but will potentially conclude that the best way to react to an oppressive government is by accepting it.

The Two outcomes described above are all, retrospectively, movements that can be classified as depressive, as the will of the individual diminishes following every attempt. It is easy to understand how those outcomes do not, in any case, promote or bring positive results to the society itself. At this point, it is easy to understand how the majority of the movements in the last 500 years brought mainly misery to their citizens.

As we mentioned above, an alternative exists for social movements that are trying to make a real change. Not every bad rebellion fails, and not every well-executed rebellion will succeed. The purpose of this book is not to arrive at conclusions regarding the correct way to create social movements, but to understand the foundation required for a social movement to construct a better system that benefits its people in case of a successful movement.

Based on our discussion, it's possible to arrive at several conclusions regarding what is necessary for the sake of the creation of a constructive movement:

- The movement should not start out of rage, anger, or frustration.
- The leader of the movement should not be alternative small groups of self-interest, like mobs or extremists.
- The main tool of the movement should not be violence.
- The movement should not promote hate and/or extremism.
- The movement should not destroy for the sake of destruction, but should destroy only as necessary.
- No abstract vision should lead the movement.

Now that we have created those guidelines, let's examine the requirements of a constructive movement:

- The movement needs to emerge out of a conscious understanding regarding the problems in society.
- The movement should articulate the problems clearly and simply.
- The action of the movement should be organized with a clear purpose.
- The leaders of the movement should be part of the populous and reflect the general wellbeing of the society.
- A deep understanding of the system's weaknesses is required to find alternatives to violence.
- The movement should benefit the people.
- A clear plan should exist regarding what needs to be changed and how to change it.
- The reconstruction plan following the success of the movement should be clear and simple to understand for the sake of the population before any action is taken.

To promise a successful constructive movement, we must answer four questions before any action is taken:

1. What is wrong in the system?
2. How can we replace it?
3. What alternative will replace it?
4. How will the alternative be constructed?

The ability of a movement to articulate those answers is the reason for the success of many leaders in history. Those questions are important, as they should build the core activity of the revolt itself. Those answers will imply practical actions necessary for the success of the revolt. The necessity to construct clear answers is not only important for the sake of the followers, but is essential to avoid actions not part of those core activities. The first two questions are important for the creation of the movement itself and the realization of the possibilities involved. The success of the revolt by itself is not enough for the movement to be constructive. In case the movement fails to rebuild a better system, a gap will be created in the governing domain which will bring violence and domination of an external elite, as discussed above.

The movement must know what alternative they'll use to replace the system for two reasons. The first is not demolishing the entire system, but keeping the best parts of the current system and not exhausting resources on the wrong targets. As any movement will require resources for demolition and then reconstruction, the resources available for the movement are, by definition, limited. The capacity to make the right move will allow the movement to save resources in both the processes of the demolition and construction, and will allow them to concentrate resources on the important problems. Understanding the future system allows for quick and efficient reconstruction of the system.

The definition of a constructive movement is a group created by the people to develop a better future for their societies. Understanding the problem, the possible realistic alternatives, the actions needed to replace the system, and clear steps for reconstruction all create a successful revolution.

How to Create Social Change

Change is a natural process fueled by trial and error. Some changes benefit humankind as individuals and as societies, and there are some that benefit only a small part of individuals without giving any benefit to the others. As this process requires errors, it should be natural to monitor the process of social evolution, looking where we've arrived and decide freely that we potentially made an error. In case such a conclusion is made, the natural process should be the destruction of the current system while keeping the positive aspects and rebuilding based on the needs of society. How can this be done?

Every conversation I've had regarding potential social changes has been opposed by a certain philosophy that concludes the masses are idiots and we're too small as individuals to create a real change. Looking at our society that way is a wonderful example of ignorance regarding the nature of social movements and the concept of society. Without any doubt, any change requires time and action. Changing the habits of one individual can take months and even years. Changing the habits and structure of a society can require years or decades if done peacefully and the right way. The right way refers to the positive outcome retrospectively.

A social movement requires several steps. The first step is the understanding and will of the individual to change their current reality. The will and understanding of an individual will not always lead to actions, but is required in case it does. Based on the history of social movements, to engage people in a social movement, it is important that:

1. The individual feels that they have a choice.
2. The individual holds a simple vision and set of rules.
3. The individual has a feeling of fairness and believes in the success of the movement itself.

Looking at the movements created in societies and nations, it can be observed that in any movement ever created there are five kinds of groups. These groups are all required for the existence and success of the movement itself. These groups are a core structure for any social movement, big or small. Understanding these groups and their connection is essential for the sake of creating and maintaining any kind of movement.

1. **Group A: The naturally idealistic philosophers.** This group has the capacity to create new ideas and is willing to practice their philosophy as long as there's a willing leader. With a leader at the head of the movement, this group of people will support and maintain movements as consultants and will support the expansion of the organization as active supporters in society.

2. **Group B: The natural leaders.** These individuals hold a range of leadership traits. From the moment a strong leader takes a clear path, the rest of the individuals participating in that group will support the system by promoting and maintaining the organization itself as subleaders of sub-movements.

3. **Group C: The anti-movement group.** This group of people actively opposes the movement. As people are hungry for information and are constantly searching for new ideas, by promoting an anti-movement, they're still promoting the ideas of the movement, but from a different angle. The more aggressive the anti-movement, the stronger the need of the followers to have an opinion. Researchers have proven that we tend to remember the surprising events of our lives. By making a movement seem abnormal or dangerous, the need of the follower to group with an extreme opinion will be created.

4. **Group D: The followers.** The followers are all the individuals that create the masses. Those individuals will follow from the moment the idea is practically constructed and existing in a way that will demand from them the minimum (as a first stage, only holding the idea and presenting it in public is sufficient). They will naturally follow. When a big enough stream of followers joins the system, the movement of the rest of the followers will naturally emerge. For this to happen, an anti-movement group is required.

5. **Group E: The passive group.** This group exists in all social movements. Most of the individuals of the previous groupings will join a movement actively. In any movement, there will be a number of individuals who naturally prefer not to participate as long as it does not come literally to their front door.

These groups create and maintain each other during the process of a social movement. Group A - represents a modest part of individuals who are aware of their society and are thinking about how to improve it. During periods in which no leader exists to actively promote and lead the new ideas, the majority of this group feel weak in both society and in government. In many cases, this group will try to live their social life with a minimal attachment to the current system, and will be called dreamers, idealist, hippies, outsiders, and so on. In all cases, it's not the first person who thought about an idea that is rewarded or thanked for its social practice, but the first person that practically tried, built, wrote, acted, or manifested the idea. In case of the arrival of a leader, Group A will actively support the leader to create the social awareness and will help attract followers.

Group B consists of individuals from Group A who have the ability to create followers. The majority of these individuals are naturally charismatic and have well-developed philosophies about society. If a leader appears without individuals of Group A to support them, the movement itself will be weak and short. As long as the leaders can engage the individuals from Group A to become followers under their leadership, the leader can create a movement. This is seen in all kinds of movements, that the power of the leader to maintain their leadership is based on the power of their advisers and executors.

Group C is a very interesting group as it is paradoxical to itself in most cases. Every change is an opportunity of leadership for a thinker from Groups A and B. But, a movement promoting anti-movement ideas to disrupt another group is just a reaction, not a true movement. The anti-movement group consists of individuals from Group A that, with the appearance of the leader from Group B, decided to protest against said movement at all cost. Because a movement can only maintain itself if both the good and bad of the movement are acknowledged, the anti-movement will inevitably help followers construct ideas, which is required for being part of the movement itself. In recent years, the leaders of the system have developed such an understanding, as they are promoting themselves in positive and negative ways for the sake of publicity. Magnificent examples of this include the campaign of Donald Trump for the presidency of the United States, and the reinforcement of the Catalan independence movement following the opposition of the Spanish government.

Group D represents the majority of society. It's important to mention that in different movements, different people will take on active or passive roles. The parameters that will engage individuals to join the group are mainly based on their knowledge in the field, the belief of the individual in the power of the movement to create change, and their willingness to sacrifice the current reality. Followers are a group, and as all groups, the capacity of the individual in the group itself diminishes to optimize his abilities in other aspects. Group D is made of individuals from Group E that decided to change the way they live for the sake of the movement. A few parameters need to exist for the individual from Group E to pass to the follower group:

- The movement must have clear structure.
- The leaders of the movement need to be acknowledged and well-known.
- The movement's platform needs to be clear and articulated in ways that will be easily repeated by the individual.

- There's a clear understanding and repetition of the purpose of the movement and how it will change the reality of the world.
- There's an active opposition group with a clear message needs to exist for the creation of opinion and social conversation.
- There's a clear understanding of what is required from the individual for joining the movement and an easy way to check whose part of the group and who isn't.

Looking back on the Nazi movement in Europe and the American movement in the Cold War, it could be assumed that the creation of a clear enemy is necessary for the creation of a strong social movement. Such an argument can be disputed under the critique that for a person to follow a vision, they only require a clear end or a clear understanding of the changes created by the movement. If that is indeed enough, the creation of an enemy for unification is a very efficient tool of fear and terror for the sake of unification, but by itself is not obligatory for a natural movement to exist. It can even be said that unless a clear enemy is knocking at the door, the creation of a far-off enemy for unification based on fear is required, only in case the movement is unnatural and unnecessary for the population itself. Violence can only bring violence and fear can only bring destruction and separation, which are not productive for the individual or for the society itself in the long-term. In many cases concerning social movements, the easy way is not the right way. It is indeed easier to scare people and separate them than it is to make them understand each other and show tolerance. In all cases, hatred built in an individual perspective for a social movement will not vanish following the success of the movement, which will reinforce a feeling of separation and a need to maintain something to hate.

As societies are changing based on the changes created by the masses themselves, it can be assumed that a movement will be successful only when the masses decide to follow it.

The fascinating point of our social order is that we all start in Group E. All groups start as passive in their societies. Individuals evolve and change, while the society around them is changing constantly in a parallel way. Looking at Western society, the majority of citizens are passive in their societies and its movements. In a society in which elite control the capacity of individuals to evolve from Group E and also monitor the evolved groups, the governing authority controls the ability of the movements inside of its societies to evolve in the first place. Such a reality is violent and antisocial, as it oppresses social change.

Social movements are the core of any social structure. Those movements are natural, necessary, and required for the people in each society to change and evolve. A few factors can manipulate the use of this knowledge. The primary manipulation is the creation of movements that don't address the problems, but rather the consequences of the problems. Another way is to push individuals to be part of a movement for the sake of it, which creates a blind following based on the social need of the individual and not their willingness to change their reality. Grouping many problems under one movement is a manipulation of the social movement concept, as it aims to group as many people as possible that come from different motives and for different purposes. A good example of this is the numerous organizations trying to fight the horrible consequences of capitalistic pursuit of profit by attacking its consequences. Organizations occupied with saving the planet (Green Peace), saving the animals (vegetarian movement), humanist movements, Occupy Wall Street, and many more are all spending their resources fighting the consequences of human trafficking, the industrial food chain, the concentration of power, and destruction of the globe, which are all outcomes of the greed that runs our lives and destroys our planet.

Understanding social movements is a tool. As such, it is

neither bad nor good. Its usage determines its values. Without any doubt, weak and ignorant populations are easier to manipulate for the sake of personal gain. The education of the population and the creation of clear, measurable standards that will be constantly monitored are required to promise effective movements that benefit the population. The key for any successful social movement is its individuals. Strong individuals will create a strong society. This is a personal responsibility we forgot about long ago, which brought us to be unable to articulate our problems and feel incapable of changing on a social scale. The purpose of a society is to benefit its individuals, the purpose of a government is to benefit its society, and the purpose of the individual in a society is to monitor and engage in benefiting the structure and activities of its government. The importance is not to make a social movement or be part of one, but which movements can and will achieve a positive social change.

Time for a Social Change

Looking back on the history of the Western world, it is easy to observe that for thousands of years, humanity lived in a similar way to previous generations. The progress made by humans in the last 300 years has changed every aspect of our lives. Those changes have affected our society, monetary system, government, and the individual's general perspective of themselves, their county, and their surroundings. There are four different developments which changed our reality. Those changes were big and relevant by themselves separately. The short period between those changes didn't give us the time to understand them nor the time to understand where they brought us. All four revolutions became an integral and inseparable part of a new era we call now reality. These changes are:

1. The rise of democracies

2. The industrial revolution
3. The rise of capitalism
4. The technological revolution

These revolutions have pushed humanity to a new era that has changed much faster than we can adapt to and grasp the changes. The reality of people born in the beginning of the 20th century, the middle, and the end of that period is so different that basic tools from older generations are no longer relevant to us. Moreover, in many cases, holding onto a system built on the old reality is so irrelevant to our needs these days that maintaining such a system is damaging and depressing the young generation. It is a fact these days, as the oldest generation lived a life that is not relevant to the existence of today and one we cannot maintain. Such a fast-changing reality created a gap of confusion that brought to power self-interested entities that maintain power by manipulating individuals' minds.

As the manipulation of the individual mind has been used for decades, the feeling of weakness in the individual's reality regarding their influence on their surroundings, the lack of knowledge regarding their basic needs of existence, combined with the isolation of the individual in a world of fear and distraction, are the main causes for the prolonging reality which we are so proud to call our life in the Western world. I believe that the problems of our generation are rooted in individuals' inability to understand and articulate the problems in their life, society, and government.

I hope and believe that reading this book has given you a deeper understanding about your life and the society around you. I hope this will give to at least a few of those who lives with those feelings and search to understand and change, the language needed. Hopefully, this language will bring us one step closer to find a solution to this twisted reality we call life.

It is time for a change, a real one. Not one based on

words, but one in which words are used to describe actions. As ideas never die, but populations do, the need for an actual change is necessary. In the 21st century, the capitalistic ideas do not require individuals for the sake of its existence. It's time to build a new system in which the individual's understanding of their role and influence in society is clear and positive. We need a system that will be so easy to understand and pass on and allow the philosophy to survive without the need for specific individuals. Thanks to the changes of the last 150 years, we have put together the foundation necessary for global cooperation that will benefit humanity. Those tools are available, used these days for the sake of the prosperity of the few and the intimidation of the many.

A society of individuals who have no understanding regarding their needs, are terrified of changes, and don't have the tools necessary for the destruction and reconstruction of the system. Such a population will be not only unable to maintain themselves for long periods, but will inevitably create a gap between the individual and their society. This gap will allow the local elite to dominate its population by the tyranny of terror and isolation. The endless good inventions have changed the way the individual sees themselves, their society, the globe, and the universe. Humans have created a way to communicate worldwide like never before, and are aware of the rest of humanity and the planet by indirect communication. The tools needed for cultivating the earth in a manner that will promise balance is available and a large access to information to all the population for education and sharing ideas exist. To admit that we have taken a bad turn does not mean that we should be punished or feel any kind of fear and guilt.

A government has its authority by the people, which it governs, and individuals must understand their power to control and shape the future for their children, land, and freedom for a healthy society. Societies, laws, and governments have emerged to create better conditions for the individual as part of a group. When the government is incapable to delivers such services for its community, it should be replaced and reconstructed for the benefit of the people.

A group is made out of its individual, just as a state is made out of its cities. The necessary change starts with the individual regarding their way of life in their house, society, city, and country. The communication channels, the fast movement of information, and the willingness of the people try to create a better society and future for their children is the essence of our ability to survive.

As long as we continue to educate our kids through doctrines of fear, self-concentration, and separation, we will never manage to take ourselves out of the fear of the past, and we will never have time to think about creating a better future. We don't need to be sorry and don't need forgiveness, as it was never theirs to give or to take. The foundation for a healthy, global world has been installed and mastered, and the tools needed for unification exist. The understanding that we are the only threat to ourselves is widely known and the will of the people for a better life exists. Changes start with small movements that create a pattern and evolve to a constant stream of evolution.

We are the only ones in charge of our future. The time to make a change is now. Churchill said a revolution of the people is required every generation. As the reality of the 21st century is constantly showing us that the current system and government is not working for the benefit of its citizen, isn't it time to start changing it?

EPILOGUE

A Different Kind of Education: The Fundamental Point of Constructive Education

As the Western society in the 21st century evolved attached to values of materialism, the need to own personal belongings for the sake of a self-image became an inseparable aspect of young generations. It can be observed in the pursuit of self-fulfillment and the need to feel control based on ownership of fashion item, cars and properties. The claim of properties as our own, under both individuals and collective is a false conception, bringing only misery and separation.

If the purpose of humans is to promote peace and prosperity, it is important to remove those falls conception from the mind of the young generation. The need and claim of proprietorship by the human race is partly, or in many cases wholly, the cause of all disturbance of peace on earth. An individual should be able to identify a place as his home, but should not fine in its pride or a reason to create destruction for others.

We are all coming from nature and sharing earth. We

required a livable earth as any other living organism on this planet. We have enough land and resources to maintain not only the human race, but all its plans and animals as a whole. With the growing global awareness and the recent technological development, it is possible today to maintain a constructive ecological system that should benefit all the living on earth without the need to corrupt the land and the nature.

Ignorant and so called civilized person are claiming proprietary right on the communal properties of nature because they have detached themselves from the nature and its inhabitant. It is impossible to find neither happiness nor peacefulness detached from our source, which is nature. The enrichment and comfort achieved in the price of the enslavement of the rest of the population, is a symptom of a general behavior. Which slowly but surely destroy the nature around us and diminish the number of species and animal on the planet.

We are all part of earth and its ecological system, ignoring it will undoubtedly bring to the destruction of our civilization, our lands and our humanity. This fundamental idea must be in the roots of any educational system, as it affects the dreams, actions and decision making of our future generations.

The points below are some general points written under the principal of constructive education. These points do not reflect an educational system, but the ideas that should stand behind it. As different societies in the world have different ways to pass information to each other, a custom educational system should be built based on the habit and norms of the local population.

- Words exist to express reality, never the opposite. By creating a reality based on words, a lack of healthy communication will arise which will bring fear, separation, and loneliness.

- The collective, as a whole, is always problematic as it is a conceptual invention. For a better society, the individual should be educated as an individual and then as a part of a realistic group.

- Knowledge is a positive power only when it comes out of peacefulness. Change is a positive thing that should be encouraged and not feared. Knowledge is positive only if an individual or a group uses it for the benefit of the future generations.

- A person is better doing one simple task at a time. A complicated task is complex for an individual if the person didn't master the simple tasks separately before putting it together, or if a person lacks the understanding of the task itself.
    - The best way to optimize an individual and a society is to outsource everything that is not the core activity of an individual, while keeping an active part in the creation process.
    - Core activities of an individual are the activities an individual like naturally, feels comfortable doing for long periods, creates an intellectual sense of existence, and those are easily understood in the individual's mind.

- There are 10 basic principles of life:
    1. Know yourself as you are.
    2. Be an example of your demands.
    3. Respect your surroundings as you ask to be respected.
    4. Take the time to understand.
    5. Accept opinions as they are all part of the same reality.
    6. Embrace the needs of your society as they are your own.
    7. Strive to be the best version of yourself.
    8. Encourage love and understanding.

9. Ask to learn and learn to ask.

10. Accept failure as it's a part of learning and success.

- To help people, an individual must focus on people's needs and dreams, not on his own.

- The educational system should lead the individual not to compare themselves to what they think they should be, but to what they were yesterday.

- A person must know how to make decisions based on their own inner true, but should live by making as few decisions as possible.

- Positive productivity means creating better quality, not creating more. For positive productivity, time and peacefulness are required.

Resources and Additional Reading

The books and references below are some of the resources that I read and studied before the writing of this book. Many other resources have contributed to the ideas and conclusions written above that I cannot recall, due to the stream of information I encountered in the last 15 years.

If YOU have any inquiries, thoughts, questions, notes, or ideas you would like to share, please feel free to contact me at any time to my personal email at the following email: amitai@backtoourselves.com.

You can also find me online:

www.Facebook.com/backtoourselves

https://backtoourselves.org/

Recommended Reading

<u>Psychology and Sociology</u>

- *Cognitive Psychology* by Robert Sternberg
- *Toward a Psychology of Being* by Abraham Maslow
- *Sapians* by Yuval Noah Harari.
- *Antifragile* by Nassim Nicholas Taleb
- *Focus* by Daniel Goleman
- *Think Fast and Slow* by Daniel Kahneman
- *Wage of Rebellion* by Chris Jedges

<u>Politics and Government</u>

- *On Politics* by Alan Ryan
- *Chronicles* by Tomas Piketty
- *The Utopia of Rules* by David Graeber
- *The Looting Machine* by Thomas Burgis
- *Why Nation Fails* by Doran Acemoalu and James A. Robinson
- *The Shock Doctrine* by Naomi Klein

<u>Economics</u>

- *The Intelligent Investor* by Benjamin Graham
- *Mania, Panics and Crashes* by Robert Z. Aliber and Charles P Kindleberger
- *Tap Dancing to Work* by Warren Buffet
- *Capital* by Karl Marx

References

<u>Violence Against Teachers</u>

- "Understanding and Preventing Violence Directed Against Teachers" - Dorothy Espelage, Eric M. Anderman, Veda Evanell Brown, Abraham, Lynne Lane, Susan D. McMahon, Linda A. Reddy Rutgers, R. Reynolds
- http://www.oecd.org/edu/innovation-education/34739292.pdf

<u>Main Causes of Death Around the World</u>

- https://www.cdc.gov/nchs/fastats/leading-causes-of-death.htm
- https://www.livescience.com/60429-global-disease-death-burden.html
- https://www.worldatlas.com/articles/top-ten-leading-causes-of-death-in-the-world.html

<u>Fear Factor by the Media</u>

- https://criminaljusticeonlineblog.com/11/terrorism-the-media-and-the-fear-factor/
- Jaehnig, Jounaid s and Trorism. Captives of the Libertarian Tradition, 53 IND. LJ. 717, 743 (1978).
- http://www.independent.co.uk/voices/manchester-attack-intelligence-leaks-nyt-freedom-of-the-press-limitations-a7755346.html

<u>Learning New Skills and Cognitive Capacity</u>

- Britton, B., & Tesser, A. (1982). Effects of prior knowledge on use of cognitive capacity in three complex cognitive tasks. Journal of Verbal Learning and Verbal Behaviour, 21, 421–436.

- Anderson, J. (1982). Acquisition of cognitive skill. Psychological Review, 89, 369–406.
- Chi, M., Glaser, R., & Rees, E. (1982). Expertise in problem solving. In R. Sternberg (Ed.), Advances in the psychology of human intelligence. NJ : Erlbaum.
- Lansman, M., & Hunt, E. (1982). Individual differences in secondary task performance. Memory and Cognition, 10, 10–24.
- Cognitive Disequilibrium, Jackie Kibler - Department of Psychology, University of Montana, Missoula, USA

Learning, Time, and Sleeping

- Universite de Montreal. "Learning to play the piano? Sleep on it!." ScienceDaily. ScienceDaily, 21 August 2014.
- *Cedernaes J. et. al. Short Sleep Makes Declarative Memories Vulnerable to Stress in Humans. *Sleep*, June 22, 2015.
- Swedish Brain Foundation, Swedish Research Council, AFA Försäkring, and Novo Nordisk Foundation. Linda Koffmar "Sleep loss makes memories less accessible in stressful situations." 2015-07-13

Enough Resources Exist for All Humanity

- We Already Grow Enough Food For 10 Billion People and Still Can't End Hunger - By Eric Holt Gimenez. https://www.huffingtonpost.com/eric-holt-gimenez/world-hunger_b_1463429.html
- The world produces enough food to feed everyone. So why do people go hungry? - Jomo Kwame Sundaram, Assistant Director-General and Coordinator for Economic and Social Development, Food and Agriculture Organization, United Nations

https://www.weforum.org/agenda/2016/07/the-world-produces-enough-food-to-feed-everyone-so-why-do-people-go-hungry

Learned Helplessness, Shock, and Responses

- Abramson, L. Y., Seligman, M. E., & Teasdale, J. D. (1978). Learned helplessness in humans: Critique and reformulation. *Journal of Abnormal Psychology, 87*(1), 49-74.

- Maier, S. F., & Seligman, M. E. (1976). Learned helplessness: Theory and evidence. *Journal of Experimental Psychology: General, 105*(1), 3-46.

- De Villiers PA. Reinforcement and response rate interaction in multiple random-interval avoidance schedules. *J Exp Anal Behav.* 1972 Nov;**18**(3):499–507.
- FLESHLER M, HOFFMAN HS. A progression for generating variable-interval schedules. *J Exp Anal Behav.* 1962 Oct;**5**:529–530.
- HERRNSTEIN RJ. Relative and absolute strength of response as a function of frequency of reinforcement. *J Exp Anal Behav.* 1961 Jul;**4**:267–272.
- Herrnstein RJ. Method and theory in the study of avoidance. *Psychol Rev.* 1969 Jan;**76**(1):49–69.
- Herrnstein RJ. On the law of effect. *J Exp Anal Behav.* 1970 Mar;**13**(2):243–266.
- Herrnstein RJ, Hineline PN. Negative reinforcement as shock-frequency reduction. *J Exp Anal Behav.* 1966 Jul;**9**(4):421–430.

The Richest People in the World and Their Values

- http://time.com/money/4746795/richest-people-in-the-world/
- https://inequality.org/facts/global-inequality/

- https://www.oxfam.org/en/pressroom/pressreleases/2017-01-16/just-8-men-own-same-wealth-half-world
- https://en.wikipedia.org/wiki/The_World%27s_Billionaires
- http://indianexpress.com/article/business/richest-people-in-the-world-bloomberg-bill-gates-warren-buffett-mark-zuckerberg-jeff-bezos-koch-brothers-2878601/

External Debts by Countries

- https://www.cia.gov/library/publications/the-world-factbook/rankorder/2079rank.html
- https://en.wikipedia.org/wiki/List_of_countries_by_external_debt
- https://en.wikipedia.org/wiki/Debt-to-GDP_ratio
- https://data.worldbank.org/indicator/GC.DOD.TOTL.GD.ZS?view=chart

ABOUT THE AUTHOR

In the last decade I had the opportunity to live and work in many countries around the world. the difference between the cultures and the governments had open my eyes to different perspectives which teach me a lot about myself and about the world that we are marching into.

I believe a better future is achievable. It requires our awareness and active cooperation. I hope to be able to promote such a social movement and lay down the foundation needed to open people's mine and perspective.

www.ingramcontent.com/pod-product-compliance
Lightning Source LLC
Chambersburg PA
CBHW060052260726
48658CB00004B/1276